PENGUIN PLAYS

LETTICE AND LOVAGE
and
YONADAB

One of the foremost dramatists of our time, Peter Shaffer was born in Liverpool and educated at St Paul's School and Trinity College, Cambridge. He had several varied jobs before earning fame as a playwright – working as a 'Bevin Boy' in the coal mines during the Second World War, in the acquisitions department of the New York Public Library and for the London music-publishing firm of Boosey & Hawkes.

His first big success came in 1958 with *Five Finger Exercise*. The play ran for nearly two years at the Comedy Theatre in London, and was subsequently presented, with great acclaim, in New York City. Other Shaffer successes include *The Private Ear: The Public Eye* (which, like *Lettice and Lovage*, starred Maggie Smith and played at the Globe Theatre); *The Royal Hunt of the Sun*, an epic drama concerning the Spanish conquest of the Inca empire; the hilarious farce *Black Comedy*; *The Battle of Shrivings*; *Equus*, a sensational triumph in London and in New York, where it received the 1975 Tony Award for Best Play of the year; and *Amadeus*, which also won the same prize, as well as the 1979 *Evening Standard* Drama Award, the *Plays and Players* Award, and the London Theatre Critics' Award. In 1984 the film of *Amadeus* won the Academy Award for both script and picture. *Lettice and Lovage* received the *Evening Standard* Drama Award for the Best Comedy of 1988. Penguin publish a number of his plays.

Peter Shaffer was awarded the CBE in the 1987 Birthday Honours List.

PETER SHAFFER

LETTICE AND LOVAGE
and
YONADAB

PENGUIN BOOKS

PENGUIN BOOKS

Published by the Penguin Group
27 Wrights Lane, London W8 5TZ, England
Viking Penguin Inc., 40 West 23rd Street, New York, New York 10010, USA
Penguin Books Australia Ltd, Ringwood, Victoria, Australia
Penguin Books Canada Ltd, 2801 John Street, Markham, Ontario, Canada L3R 1B4
Penguin Books (NZ) Ltd, 182–190 Wairau Road, Auckland 10, New Zealand

Penguin Books Ltd, Registered Offices: Harmondsworth, Middlesex, England

Lettice and Lovage first published by André Deutsch 1988
Published with revisions by Penguin Books 1989
Yonadab first published by Penguin Books 1989
10 9 8 7 6 5 4 3 2

Made and printed in Great Britain by
Cox and Wyman Ltd, Reading, Berks.
Filmset in Linotron Bembo by
Rowland Phototypesetting Ltd, Bury St Edmunds, Suffolk

CONTENTS

PREFACE

Both of these plays have been rewritten, *Yonadab* extensively, *Lettice and Lovage* only slightly, yet still significantly.

Yonadab was inspired directly by Dan Jacobson's fine novel *The Rape of Tamar*. I first encountered this book in 1970, and it produced in me an almost instant desire to animate the story through actors. Part of that desire was to bring to theatrical life the startling invention whereby Yonadab spies on Amnon and his sister in their bed and witnesses for himself the fruit of his plotting: the shaming of the House of David. Part also was to write a play that could avoid the clichés of biblical drama and, at the same time, explore and express my own feelings about one of the few unavoidable texts in the world – that blood-spattered chronicle of death and deception, racial arrogance and magnificence known as the Old Testament.

As I worked on the material it moved continuously further away from Jacobson's brilliantly cool narrative. The plot writhed and twisted convulsively into new patterns, and Yonadab himself, on a hint in the novel, changed radically. I became obsessed by the figure of a cynic lured for a moment into the possibility of Belief: an anguished figure forever caught between the impossibility of religious credo and the equal impossibility of perpetual incredulity.

The first production of the play at the National Theatre in 1985, directed by Peter Hall with Alan Bates in the name part, was not complete. In the scurrying days of rehearsal the text was really still evolving in my head, freeing itself from many constraints, striving day by day to achieve an ever greater clarity and credibility. It was given (as is the generous and sensible habit of the National) a long rehearsal period, but that was not long enough.

Another six months would not have been long enough, because in truth the play was not yet ripe. Bates in particular was tirelessly gallant in struggling to animate it; the Company followed him bravely; the set of John Bury – a vast, translucent pavilion covered with Hebrew writing from the Book of Samuel, which narrated the story even as at times it shadowed and slid over the performers – was finely original, but it was all to no avail. The piece itself, even with the expert direction of Hall, remained opaque.

Now I think it is ready to be seen. I present here a text that is radically changed. Although its general shape and intention remain the same, at least 80 per cent of the dialogue has been rewritten. The story has been made clearer; the action has been given greater tension and texture; the characters have all been strengthened in the drawing. Most of all, the appearance of six Helpers in white anonymity provides a radically new formulation for the entire play. These protean Assistants help to lubricate the works of the piece and, at the same time, lend it both a remoteness and an immediacy that should generate a special atmosphere for its events to live in.

I would like to stress that this is very much a reading version of the play. Its New York production (which, it is hoped, will be its next English-speaking one) is still several months away, and rehearsals are bound to alter details of both dialogue and action. When the word is made flesh, the flesh is liable to change the word. However, the present pages represent substantially the play I intend and in which I now feel a truly excited confidence.

Yonadab exists in a world of superstition, of prophecies, interlocking dreams and the deep-running insistence of Semitic fear and wilfulness. It is a world of desert and judgement: the limitless void of sand and the exact limitation of the Law. This new stylization should help to make it come alive with an exact and extraordinary vividness.

The rewriting of *Lettice and Lovage* has been far less radical, being composed on a text that, as I write, has already been played at the Globe Theatre for a year without a single empty seat. In the original – played so marvellously by Maggie Smith and Margaret Tyzack – the two ladies were left preparing to blow up a select list of buildings they most detested with a medieval weapon. This fantastic climax produced much laughter – but I was always aware of how strenuously it had been added on to the play in order to achieve just that effect. It was really a forced scene, dismissing the piece into improbability. Over the ensuing months I came to disapprove of it for this reason and spent much time considering other endings more natural and organic. Finally the present one occurred, which seems to me to be both correct and pleasing. It is also, in our lunatic world, all too credible. I look to see a variant of E.N.D. Tours advertised in the *Sunday Times* any week now.

When it first appeared there were some critics, both lay and professional, who did not want a happy ending to the play at all. However, I believe most firmly that an unhappy one is actually a betrayal of the genre of comedy. For the life of me, I could not leave Lettice weeping in a basement.

Now with this rewrite she prospers, and Lotte prospers with her, and their progenitor is pleased. So also are their re-reviewers. And so – very much so, apparently – are their audiences. A happy ending indeed.

Peter Shaffer
December 1988

LETTICE AND LOVAGE

A Comedy in Three Acts

To Leo
who asked for a comedy
and
For Maggie
who incarnates comedy
with love

CHARACTERS

LETTICE DOUFFET

SURLY MAN

LOTTE SCHOEN

MISS FRAMER

MR BARDOLPH

VISITORS TO FUSTIAN HOUSE

*

The action of the play takes place in the Grand Hall of Fustian House, Wiltshire; Miss Schoen's office at the Preservation Trust, Architrave Place, London; and Miss Douffet's basement flat, Earl's Court.

First performed at the Theatre Royal, Bath, on 6 October 1987, and subsequently at the Globe Theatre, London W1, under the management of Robert Fox Ltd, the Shubert Organization and Roger Berlind, with the following cast:

LETTICE DOUFFET Maggie Smith
SURLY MAN Bruce Bennett
LOTTE SCHOEN Margaret Tyzack
MISS FRAMER Joanna Doubleday
MR BARDOLPH Richard Pearson
VISITORS TO FUSTIAN HOUSE Alex Allenby, Joanna Doubleday, Jennifer Lautrec, Barbara Lewis, Maxine McFarland, Lindsay Rodwell, Shelagh Stuttle, Nick Sampson

DIRECTOR Michael Blakemore
DESIGN Alan Tagg
COSTUMES Susan Yelland
LIGHTING Robert Bryan

ACT ONE

SCENE 1: A

Elizabethan music: lugubrious.

Curtain rises on the Grand Hall of Fustian House: a dim sixteenth-century hall hung with dim portraits of the Fustian family.

The main feature is an imposing Tudor staircase of oak which descends into the middle of it. A scarlet rope is stretched across the bottom, denying access to the public.

Standing near this object is MISS LETTICE DOUFFET, *the guide appointed by the Preservation Trust to show people round this gloomy old house. She is a lady in middle life. At this moment she is striving valiantly to suppress her own natural exuberance, and deliver herself dutifully of the text she is employed to recite, and which she has memorized.*

Behind her stands a motley group of tourists – as many as can be managed – who for the most part look downcast and bored. It is a grey rainy day, and the house is freezing.

LETTICE: We come now to the most remarkable feature of Fustian House. This is the Grand Staircase, constructed in 1560 out of Tudor oak. It consists of fifteen stairs, made from planks cut at the neighbouring saw-mill of Hackton. The banister displays an ogival pattern typical of the period. The plaster ceiling above is embellished with a design of love-knots, also typical.

(*All look up without interest. A man yawns. A woman looks at her watch.*)

Please note the escutcheons placed at intervals around the cornice. These bear the family motto in Latin: *Lapsu surgo* – meaning, 'By a fall I rise.' This alludes to an incident which

occurred on the Feast of Candlemas 1585 upon this actual staircase. On that night Queen Elizabeth the First, making a Royal Progress through her realm, chose to honour with her presence the yeoman merchant John Fustian. To mark the occasion Fustian caused a banquet to be laid here in this hall, and himself stood by the Queen's side at the top of the stairs to escort her down to it. However, as Her Majesty set foot on the first stair she tripped on the hem of her elaborate dress, and would have fallen, had not her host taken hold of her arm and saved her. The Queen being in merry mood immediately called for a sword and dubbed him a Knight of Her Realm.
(*The man yawns again, loudly. Others also yawn.*)
This concludes the tour of Fustian House. On behalf of the Preservation Trust I wish you a good afternoon.

THE PUBLIC: (*Drowsily*) Good afternoon . . .
(*They file past her dispiritedly.* LETTICE *looks after them in dejection. The light fades and the lugubrious music returns. The crowd of tourists walks around the stage, shedding outer garments, reversing them or putting on new ones.*)

SCENE 1: B

Lights up again. It is some days later: a little brighter weather. LETTICE *stands just as before, with a new group of listeners – the same people with different hats, scarves and glasses – but equally bored. Among them is a young husband and wife; the wife carries a baby in a sling.* LETTICE *herself is bored, and recites her text in a mechanical monotone, much faster than before.*

LETTICE: We come now to the most remarkable feature of Fustian House. This is the Grand Staircase constructed in 1560 out of Tudor oak. It consists of fifteen stairs, made from planks cut at the neighbouring saw-mill of Hackton. The banister displays an ogival pattern typical of the period. The plaster ceiling above is embellished with a design of love-knots, also typical.

(*All look up as before, without interest. A man scratches himself. A woman coughs.* LETTICE *presses on desperately.*)
Please note the escutcheons placed at intervals around the cornice. These bear the family motto in Latin: *Lapsu surgo* – meaning, 'By a fall I rise.' This alludes to an incident which occurred on the Feast of Candlemas 1585–
(*The baby suddenly starts crying. The mother tries to hush it. All the tourists crowd around it in concern.* LETTICE *is ignored.*)
(*With sudden ardour, making up her mind*) *Please!* You are looking in fact at a unique monument of English History! Yes, indeed. And one of the most romantic . . . It is known as the *Staircase of Advancement*! . . . Does anyone know why it is so called?
(*They stare at her in silence. One or two shake their heads and murmur, 'No.'*)
I will tell you. On that day of Candlemas – which by the way has nothing to do with Christmas as some of you may think, but falls on the second day of February – John Fustian gave a great feast in this hall to honour Queen Elizabeth. We do not know what he served at this banquet, but no doubt it contained hedgehogs.
(*The scratching man is startled. A woman cries out in disgust.*)

THE MAN: Hah?

LETTICE: Certainly. Hedgehogs were a considerable delicacy in those days. They were known as 'urchins' and would have been endored. Do you know what that word means – 'endored'?
(*The crowd murmurs, 'No.'*)
Made golden! Glazed with egg yolk. An exquisite word, do you not think? . . . They were imaginative, our ancestors, in what they ate. Their food is a particular enthusiasm of mine. (*To a woman*) Do you know they also ate puffins?

THE WOMAN: Good heavens!

LETTICE: They classified them as fish so they could eat them on Fast Days of the Church. Clever, you see. The same with coney – similarly classified. You know what coneys are?

THE WOMAN: I'm afraid I don't . . . Pine cones, perhaps?

LETTICE: No, no, no – much juicier! (*Conspiratorially*) Infant rabbit – torn from its mother's breast. Or cut from her womb.

THE WOMAN: Oh no!

LETTICE: The Romans called them *lauraces*, and they were reputedly delicious.

THE WOMAN: How disgusting!

LETTICE: We are in no position to find other ages disgusting, I fancy. I resume my story . . . Her Majesty arrived for John Fustian's feast, emerging from the bedchamber at the head of the stairs. She was wearing a dazzling dress with a hem on to which had been sewn one hundred pearls, dredged from the Indian Ocean, and sent as a present by an Ottomite Sultan! Alas, so heavy was this hem that she tripped on the first step and would have fallen the whole way down, had not her host – who was standing in the middle of the staircase – on the seventh stair from the top, can you see it? –

(*All peer upwards and murmur 'Yes!' They are now interested.*)

– had he not rushed up and caught her in the very nick of time. For this service the Queen immediately called for a sword and dubbed him her Knight! She then tore off the six largest pearls from her treacherous hem and bade him set them in the handle of the sword which had just ennobled him. (*Pause.*) You would have seen that sword in the next room, couched on a bed of crimson velvet, but unfortunately it was stolen last week. An interesting story, is it not?

HER HEARERS: (*Agreeing, pleased*) Oh yes! . . . Yes, indeed . . . Charming . . .

LETTICE: Thank you very much.

HER HEARERS: Thank *you*!

LETTICE: This concludes the tour of Fustian House. On behalf of the Preservation Trust, I wish you a good afternoon.

HER HEARERS: (*Gratefully*) Good afternoon.

(*She smiles at them happily. The lights fade, as sprightlier Elizabethan music springs up. Yet again the tourists move around the stage, changing their clothes.*)

SCENE 1: C

Lights up again. Music fades. It is again some days later: brighter yet. LETTICE, *as before, is lecturing another group of the public – but this time it is clearly a pleased and spellbound audience. Her own manner is also now confident and happily dramatic. Only one man in the group, standing a little apart – a surly-looking creature in a cap and raincoat – is growing increasingly suspicious and restive as her recital goes on.*

LETTICE: You are looking now at what is indisputably the most famous staircase in England! . . . *The Staircase of Aggrandizement!* On the night of February the Second, 1585 – a brilliant snowy night – John Fustian laid before his Sovereign here in this hall a monumental feast! The tables were piled high with hedgehogs, puffins and coneys! Also herons, peacocks and swans! Each of them was waiting to be carved in its own particular manner. (*To the group*) Did you know there was a different word for the way you carved each bird?
(*Murmurs of 'No!'*)
Oh yes! You *disfigured* a peacock, but you *lifted* a swan! Nothing could exceed in diversity or succulence an Elizabethan feast – and on the night we speak of – in this room – a hundred of the liveliest courtiers stood salivating to consume it! (*Increasingly excited by her tale*) Suddenly she appeared – Gloriana herself, the Virgin Queen of England! – in a blaze of diamonds presented to her by the Tsar Ivan the Terrible, who had seen a portrait of her in miniature, and lost a little of his icy heart to her chaste looks! Smiling, she set foot upon the first stair, up there! Alas, as she did so – at that precise moment – she slipped and would have plunged headlong down all fifteen polished and bruising steps, had not her host – standing precisely where I stand now, *at the very bottom – leapt in a single bound* the whole height of the staircase to where she stood, and saved her!
(*One or two gasp with amazement.*)
Imagine the scene! Time as if suspended! A hundred beribboned guests frozen like Renaissance statues: arms outstretched in powerless gesture! Eyes wide with terror in the

flare of torches! . . . And then suddenly John Fustian moves! He who up to that moment has lived his whole life as a dull and turgid yeoman, breaks the spell! Springs forward – upward – rises like a bird – like feathered Mercury – *soars* in one astounding leap the whole height of these stairs, and at the last possible moment catches her in his loyal arms, raises her high above his head, and rose-cheeked with triumph cries up to her: 'Adored Majesty! Adored and *En*dored Majesty! Fear not! You are safe! – And your hedgehogs await!'

(This recital produces a reaction of pure joy in her hearers, some of whom actually applaud. The SURLY-LOOKING MAN, *however, is not impressed. He speaks in a whine of hostility.)*

SURLY MAN: Excuse me.

LETTICE: Yes?

SURLY MAN: Could you give me your reference for that story?

LETTICE: My what?

SURLY MAN: Reference. I'm by the way of being an Elizabethan scholar. The doings of the Virgin Queen constitute my hobby. I have nowhere read that John Fustian leapt up that staircase, let alone lifted her on high or spoke those words.

LETTICE: It is true nevertheless.

SURLY MAN: I don't see how it can be.

LETTICE: What do you say?

SURLY MAN: It's really impossible to leap those stairs from a standing position. There are fifteen of them.

LETTICE: I know how many there are. *I* told *you.*

SURLY MAN: Well then.

LETTICE: I'm not quite sure what you mean by 'well then'.

SURLY MAN: Well then it's impossible. Your story is, frankly, not on.

(Pause.)

I ask you again, please, for your reference.

(Pause.)

LETTICE: Excuse me, but there is a hostility in your voice which implies that what I am saying is an untruth. That it is lacking in veracity.

SURLY MAN: It's lacking in possibility, that's what it's lacking in.

It can't be done. You can't do a standing leap straight up in the air from here, and land on the fifteenth step of a staircase. An Olympic athlete couldn't do it.

LETTICE: (*A little flustered*) Well . . . it might be an exaggeration, I'm willing to grant you that. The Chronicle says 'in a single bound' but it may just be using a figure of poetic speech. You as an Elizabethan scholar know there was a certain use of lyrical exaggeration in the courtly prose of the sixteenth century. A 'single bound' might indeed have been in reality two, three or even four single bounds. But the heroism of the act – the sheer exuberant romance of it – *leaps* from the pages of the Chronicle I quote as dazzlingly as John Fustian did himself!

SURLY MAN: (*Implacably*) Yes, but what is it? That's all I'm asking. What is it, please?

LETTICE: What is what?

SURLY MAN: The Chronicle you quote.

LETTICE: The Family Chronicle, of course. The Fustian Family Chronicle!

SURLY MAN: And where may I find that?

LETTICE: You mayn't.

SURLY MAN: Why not?

LETTICE: Because it is not published. It lies hidden in a private archive. Safe from the eyes of those who would use it for aggressive and uncharitable purposes.

(*The others murmur with approval. Sounds of 'Hear! Hear!' 'That's right', etc. They look at the* SURLY MAN *with dislike.*)

This tour is now at an end. Please take that way out. As you go you will observe a saucer on the maplewood table by the door. It is from the very first period of the Wedgwood factory: hence its delicate shape and shade. Its purpose is for the collection of such (*elaborate accent*) *pourboires* as you may care to leave. If, as is possible, some of you lack the French tongue, I translate that word as –

SURLY MAN: Tips.

LETTICE: (*Sweetly*) Tokens of appreciation.

(*She smiles with sweetness at him. He marches off crossly. The others thank* LETTICE *effusively, shaking her hand or warmly saying goodbye as the lights fade.*)

SCENE 1: D

Lively music. The crowd of tourists again mills around the stage, deftly changing into summer attire. Lights up. A brilliant day.

The same scene as before. LETTICE *again lecturing, very much in control: her public listen attentively and enthralled. To one side, holding a guidebook, stands* LOTTE SCHOEN*: a severe-looking lady in her late forties, her dark hair and dress both aggressively plain.*

LETTICE: The incident I have just described to you – in which the Virgin Queen Elizabeth was saved from almost certain death by a feat of daring completely unachievable today *by even the greatest Olympic athlete* – is only one of many deeds of high drama which have been enacted upon the stage of this historic staircase. (*Pause.*) Not all of them, alas, were so happy in their outcome. The ensuing century was in every way darker, and the doings on its staircases were correspondingly more murky. It was upon these very stairs in the reign of William and Mary, that the most *terrible* of all events connected with this house occurred – on Midsummer morning, sixteen hundred and eighty-nine.
(*All look expectant.* LETTICE *warms to her tale.*)
This day was intended to celebrate the marriage of Miss Arabella Fustian to the handsomest young lordling in the region. The bride was a radiantly beautiful girl of eighteen – 'the catch of the County', as she was called. On the morning of her wedding her father, Sir Nicholas, stood exactly where I stand now – waiting to escort his only daughter to the church. The door of the bedchamber opened above –
(*She points: all look eagerly.*)
– and out stepped this exquisite creature in a miasma of white samite. It is not hard to imagine her father staring up at her, tears welling in his old eyes – she about to descend these stairs for the last time a maiden! And then – ah, suddenly! a terrible drumming is heard! A frantic pounding along the oak gallery – and towards her, galloping at full speed, is Charger, the faithful mastiff of the family, wild with excitement at smell-

ing the nuptial baked meats roasting in the kitchen below! In his hurtling frenzy he knocks the girl aside. She staggers – flails the air – shoots out her hand for the banister, which alas is too far from her, and *falls headlong* after the beast! . . . her lovely body rolling like a cloud down the fifteen stairs you see, until at last with one appalling jolt it comes to rest at her father's feet! . . . (*She points to the spot, at her own.*) No Mercury he, but ancient and arthritic, he stoops to touch her. Is she dead? No, the Saints be praised! Her neck is unbroken. (*A pause.*) In a dreadful echo of the gesture with which his ancestor won the family title, he catches the girl up in his arms and, watched by the agonized dog, carries her upwards to her room. A room she was never to leave again. Arabella regained consciousness, yes, but her legs, which had danced the gavotte and the coranto as no legs had ever danced them, were now twisted beneath her in mockery of the love-knots which grace the plaster ceiling above you!

(*All look up.*)

By her own choice the girl immured herself in that chamber up there for life, receiving no visitors but howling incessantly the Marriage Hymn which had been specially composed for her by Henry Purcell himself! . . . The Family Chronicle records that her attendants were all likewise distorted. I quote it for you. 'The wretched lady would employ as domestics only those who were deformed in the legs and haunches: knotted women, bunchbacks, swivel-hips, and such as had warpage and osseous misalignment of the limbs.' Cripples of all shapes clawed their way daily up this staircase, which was now known no longer as The Staircase of Ennoblement, but the *Staircase of Wound and Woe*! This name it has retained ever since.

(*A pause.* LOTTE *finally speaks, unable to restrain herself any longer.*)

LOTTE: This is intolerable.

LETTICE: I beg your pardon.

LOTTE: I find this absolutely intolerable!

LETTICE: I'm sorry? I don't understand.

LOTTE: Miss Douffet, is it not?

LETTICE: That is my name, yes.

LOTTE: Yes! Well I would like to speak to you at once, please – in private.

LETTICE: On what subject?

LOTTE: I said private, please.

LETTICE: I find this extremely odd. I am not used to having my tours interrupted with uncivil demands.

LOTTE: (*To the public*) Would you please excuse us now? It is most urgent that I speak to this lady alone. The tour is at an end at this point anyway, I believe.

LETTICE: It is. But its conclusion is a graceful adieu, not an abrupt dismissal. And it is spoken by me.

LOTTE: I'm sorry but I really have to insist. (*To the public*) Please forgive me, but I do have the most imperative business with this lady.
(*She looks at them hard, and her look is very intimidating.*)
Please.
(*They stir uneasily.*)

LETTICE: (*To the public*) Well – it seems I have to let you go – regrettably without ceremony. What can be so urgent as to preclude manners I cannot imagine! I do hope you have all enjoyed yourselves.
(*Murmurs of enthusiastic assent: 'Oh yes!' . . . 'Thank you!' . . .*)
The way out is over there. You will find placed by the exit a Staffordshire soup bowl into which, if you care to, you may deposit such tokens of appreciation as you feel inclined to give. Thank you and goodbye.

THE PUBLIC: Goodbye, Miss . . . Goodbye . . . Thank you . . .
(*They go out, bewildered and extremely curious, looking back at the two ladies. As the last one disappears,* LOTTE*'s manner becomes even colder.*)

LOTTE: You are not permitted to receive tips, I believe.

LETTICE: I do not regard them as that.

LOTTE: What then?

LETTICE: What I called them. Some people are appreciative in this world. They warm to the thrilling and romantic aspects of our great History.

LOTTE: Others, however, warm to accuracy, Miss Douffet. And

others again – a few – are empowered to see that they receive it.

LETTICE: I don't understand you.

LOTTE: Myself, for example. My name is Miss Schoen, and I work for the Preservation Trust. In the personnel department.

(*A pause.*)

LETTICE: Oh.

LOTTE: Reports have been coming in steadily for some time now of bizarre inaccuracies in your tour here. Gross departures from fact and truth. I have myself today heard with my own ears a generous sample of what you have been giving the public, and every one of those reports falls far short of what you are actually doing. I can hardly think of one statement you made in my presence that is correct.

LETTICE: The gastronomic references for a start. They are all correct. I would like you to know I am an expert in Elizabethan cuisine.

LOTTE: (*Crisply*) I am not talking about the gastronomic references – which in any case form no part of your official recital. Today I listened to a farrago of rubbish unparalleled, I should say, by anything ever delivered by one of our employees. The whole story of John Fustian's leap upstairs, for example, concluding with his actually feeding fried hedgehogs into Queen Elizabeth's mouth directly from his fingers. As for the tale of Arabella Fustian – that is virtually fabrication from beginning to end. The girl was crippled by a fall, certainly, but it is not known how she fell. Her engagement was broken off but it is not known why, or who broke it. And so far from staying in her room singing thereafter, she lived to become a respected figure in the vicinity, noted for her work among the poor. The composer Henry Purcell was not, to my knowledge, involved in her life in any way.

(*A long pause.*)

Well? . . . What do you have to say?

LETTICE: I'm sorry – but I cannot myself get beyond your own behaviour.

LOTTE: Mine?

LETTICE: What you have just done.

LOTTE: I don't understand.

LETTICE: What you have done here, Miss Schoen, today. I don't mean your rudeness in interrupting my talk, unpleasant as that was. I mean coming here at all in the way you have. Pretending to join my group as a simple member of the public. I find that quite despicable.

LOTTE: I beg your pardon?

LETTICE: Deceitful and despicable. It is the behaviour, actually, of a spy.

LOTTE: Well, that is what I am. I came here with that specific intention. To observe unnoticed what you were doing.

LETTICE: To spy.

LOTTE: To do my duty.

LETTICE: Duty?!

LOTTE: Precisely. My duty . . . The precise and appropriate word.

LETTICE: To embarrass your employees – that is your duty? To creep about the Kingdom with a look of false interest, guidebook in hand – and then pounce on them before the people in their charge? . . . Is that how you conceive your duty – to humiliate subordinates?

LOTTE: This is a sidetrack.

LETTICE: It is not. It really is not!

LOTTE: A total sidetrack and you know it! *My* behaviour is not the issue here. Yours – *yours* is what we are discussing! It is that which needs explaining! You will report tomorrow afternoon at my office in London. I believe you know the address. Fourteen, Architrave Place. Three o'clock, if you please.

LETTICE: (*Alarmed*) Report? . . . For what? Report? . . . I don't understand. What do you mean?

(*Pause.*)

LOTTE: (*Coldly*) I suggest you now attend to the next group of tourists awaiting you. And that you confine yourself strictly to the information provided by the Trust. I will see you at three tomorrow. Good afternoon.

(*She goes out.* LETTICE *stands, appalled.*)

LETTICE: (*Calling after her, in rising panic*) I . . . I'm to be tried,

then? . . . I'm to be judged? . . . Haled to Judgment?
(*A pause.* MISS SCHOEN *has gone.*)
(*In dismay*) Oh dear.
(*A grim music. Lights fade.*)

SCENE 2

Miss Schoen's office at the Preservation Trust in London. The following afternoon.

At the back a central door. On the walls are framed posters of some of the great houses owned by the Trust. There are chairs. At her desk sits MISS SCHOEN *looking darkly through a pile of letters. There is also an official file on display. Three o'clock sounds from Big Ben outside.*

There is a faint knocking on the door.

LOTTE: (*Sharply*) Yes?
(*The faint noise continues: more sharply.*)
Yes?! Is there anyone there?
(*The knock sounds louder.*)
Yes. Come *in*!
(*The door opens timidly.* MISS FRAMER *comes in: a nervous, anxious assistant, frightened, breathy and refined.*)

FRAMER: (*A whisper*) It's me, Miss Schoen.

LOTTE: What?

FRAMER: (*Louder*) It's me, Miss Schoen.

LOTTE: Miss Framer, I do wish you could learn to knock audibly. Not scratch at the door, or fumble at it like some kind of rodent.

FRAMER: I'm sorry, Miss Schoen.
(LOTTE *raps sharply on the desk, four times.*)

LOTTE: That is a knock! Do you understand?

FRAMER: Yes, Miss Schoen.

LOTTE: Then copy it. Alert me to the fact that you wish to enter.

FRAMER: Yes, Miss Schoen.

LOTTE: Now what is it?

FRAMER: (*A whisper*) Miss Douffet is here to see you.
LOTTE: What?
FRAMER: (*Louder*) Miss Douffet is here to see you.
LOTTE: Ah.
FRAMER: I asked her to wait.
LOTTE: That was enterprising of you.
FRAMER: Thank you . . .
LOTTE: How does she seem to be?
FRAMER: Bold, I would say.
LOTTE: Bold?
FRAMER: Her clothes are bold . . . Well, bolder than mine anyway.
LOTTE: I see . . . Did you have a talk with Mr Green about her, as I asked you to?
FRAMER: Oh yes, indeed.
LOTTE: He did the original hiring, I understand.
FRAMER: Yes, that's right.
LOTTE: Well? And?
FRAMER: He says when he met her for the first time this spring he thought she might make a valuable addition to our staff of guides. She appeared to be mad on history.
LOTTE: Just mad would seem to be more like it, judging from these letters.
FRAMER: Oh dear . . .
LOTTE: Does he know nothing about her at all?
FRAMER: Nothing whatever, it seems.
LOTTE: Well, this file is worse than useless. It just gives her address and nothing else. (*Consulting it*) Nineteen, Rastridge Road, Earl's Court . . . Do you know it?
FRAMER: I'm afraid not.
LOTTE: A singularly dreary street. What I would term Victorian Varicose.
FRAMER: (*Laughing sycophantically*) Oh that's good! That's very good, Miss Schoen. Victorian Varicose! Oh, yes, indeed. Most amusing!
LOTTE: (*Ignoring the flattery*) But if she's a Londoner, what is she doing working in Wiltshire?
FRAMER: I think it was the only position available . . . Apparently

Fustian House isn't particularly popular with our guides . . . It was just for the summer.

LOTTE: I see . . . (*Suddenly touching her head*) Oh, God . . .

FRAMER: (*Fussing*) What? What is it?

LOTTE: Nothing.

FRAMER: Is it one of your headaches?

LOTTE: (*Brisk*) No.

FRAMER: Is there anything at all I can do?

LOTTE: No, thank you.

FRAMER: Perhaps an aspirin. Shall I get you an aspirin, Miss Schoen?

LOTTE: Nothing, thank you. Stop fussing! If you want to help, bring me a cup of tea. Strong.

FRAMER: Of course!

LOTTE: And one for that woman out there. She's going to need it.

FRAMER: Yes, Miss Schoen.

LOTTE: Show her in, please.

FRAMER: Yes . . . Yes . . . At once . . . I'm sorry.

(MISS FRAMER *goes out.* LOTTE *shakes some cologne from a little bottle on to a handkerchief and applies it to her temples. After a moment four loud knocks are heard and* MISS FRAMER *shows in* LETTICE DOUFFET. *She is wearing a black beret and a theatrical black cloak like some medieval abbot. She carries a leather satchel and is very uneasy.*)

LOTTE: Ah, Miss Douffet: good afternoon. Please sit down.

(LETTICE *sits in a chair facing* LOTTE.)

I hope you had a pleasant journey up to London.

LETTICE: That is not very likely, is it? – Considering one is about to be arraigned.

LOTTE: I'm sorry?

LETTICE: I'm at the Bar of Judgment, am I not?

LOTTE: Your position is to be reviewed, actually. I'm sure you see the inevitability of that. I have no choice in the matter.

LETTICE: Like the headsman.

LOTTE: I'm sorry.

LETTICE: The headsman always asked forgiveness of those he was about to decapitate.

LOTTE: I would really appreciate it if we could exclude historical analogies from this conversation.

LETTICE: As you please.

LOTTE: It is after all solely to do with your job, and your fitness to perform it. We both know what we have to talk about. As an official of the Department which employs you I cannot possibly overlook what I witnessed yesterday afternoon. I cannot understand it, and I cannot possibly condone it. Do you have anything to say in extenuation?
(*A pause.*)

LETTICE: It is not my fault.

LOTTE: I'm sorry?

LETTICE: Except in a most limited sense of that word.

LOTTE: Then whose is it?

LETTICE: I respect accuracy in recounting history when it is moving and startling. Then I would not dream of altering a single detail.

LOTTE: That is gracious of you.

LETTICE: In some cases, however, I do confess I feel the need to take a hand . . . I discovered this need working at Fustian House this summer. It is wholly the fault of that house that I yielded to it.

LOTTE: Of the house?

LETTICE: Yes.

LOTTE: You are actually blaming the house for those grotesque narrations?

LETTICE: I am. Most definitely. Fustian House is quite simply the *dullest house in England*! If it has any rival in that category I have yet to discover it . . . It is actually *impossible* to make interesting! Not only is its architecture in the very gloomiest style of Tudor building – *Nothing whatever happened in it! – over four hundred years!* A Queen almost fell downstairs – but didn't. A girl did fall – not even downstairs – and survived to be honoured by the poor. How am I expected to make anything out of that?

LOTTE: You are not expected to make things *out* of the house, Miss Douffet. Merely to show people *round* it.

LETTICE: I'm afraid I can't agree. I am there to enlighten them. That first of all.

LOTTE: Enlighten?

LETTICE: Light them up! 'Enlarge! Enliven! Enlighten!' That was my mother's watchword. She called them the three Es. She was a great teacher, my mother.

LOTTE: Really? At what institution?

LETTICE: The oldest and best. The Theatre.

(MISS SCHOEN *bristles.*)

All good actors are instructors, as I'm sure you realize.

LOTTE: (*Cold*) I'm afraid I don't at all.

LETTICE: But certainly! 'Their subject is Us – Their sources are Themselves!' – Again, my mother's phrase. She ran a touring company of players, all trained by her to speak Shakespeare thrillingly in the French tongue.

LOTTE: The French?

LETTICE: Yes. She moved to France after the war, unable to find employment in her native England equal to her talent. We lived in an agricultural town in the Dordogne. It was not really very appreciative of Shakespeare.

LOTTE: The French peasantry is hardly noted for that kind of enthusiasm, I understand.

LETTICE: Nor the intellectuals either. Voltaire called Shakespeare *barbare*, did you know that? Barbarian.

LOTTE: I'm not surprised. The Gallic mind imagines it invented civilization.

LETTICE: My mother set out to correct that impression. Her company was called, in pure defiance, 'Les Barbares'!

LOTTE: She was evidently not afraid of challenge.

LETTICE: Never! Every girl was trained to phrase faultlessly.

LOTTE: And every man also, one presumes.

LETTICE: There were no men.

LOTTE: You mean it was an all-girl company?

LETTICE: Indeed. My mother married a Free French soldier in London called Douffet, who abandoned her within three months of the wedding. She had no pleasure thereafter in associating with Frenchmen. 'They are all fickle,' she used to say. 'Fickle and furtive.'

LOTTE: A fair description of the whole nation, I would say.

LETTICE: She brought me up entirely by herself. Mainly on the road. We played all over the Dordogne – in farmhouses and barns, wherever they would have us. We performed only the history plays of Shakespeare – because history was my mother's passion. I was the stage manager, responsible for costumes, props and historical detail. She herself was famous for her Richard III. She used to wear a pillow on her back as a hump. It was brilliantly effective. No one who heard it will ever forget the climax of her performance – the cry of total despair wrung from her on the battlefield: 'Un cheval! Un cheval! Mon royaume pour un cheval!'

(LOTTE *stares, astounded.*)

All the translations were her own.

LOTTE: (*Drily*) A remarkable achievement.

LETTICE: Not for her. Language was her other passion. As I grew up I was never permitted to read anything but the grandest prose. 'Language alone frees one,' she used to say. 'And History gives one place.' She was adamant I should not lose my English Heritage, either of words or deeds. Every night she enacted for me a story from our country's past – fleshing it out with her own marvellous virtuosity! Richard's battle-field with the crown hung up in the thornbush! King Charles the First going to his execution on a freezing January morning – putting on two shirts lest when he trembled from cold his enemies should think it was from fear! *Wonderful!* . . . On a child's mind the most tremendous events were engraved as with diamond on a window pane. And to me, my tourists – simply random holidaymakers in my care for twenty minutes of their lives – are *my* children in this respect. It is my duty to enlarge them. Enlarge – enliven – enlighten them.

LOTTE: With fantasies?

LETTICE: Fantasy floods in where fact leaves a vacuum.

LOTTE: Another saying of your mother's?

LETTICE: My own! . . . When I first went to Fustian House I spoke nothing *but* fact! Exactly what was set down for me by your office – in all its glittering excitement. By the time I'd finished, my whole group would have turned grey with indifference! I myself turned grey every afternoon, just speaking it! Fustian is a haunted house – I came to realize that very quickly. Haunted by the Spirit of Nullity! Of *Nothing Ever Happening*! . . . It had to be fought!

LOTTE: With untruth.

LETTICE: With anything!

LOTTE: (*Implacably*) With untruth.

LETTICE: (*Grandly*) I am the daughter of Alice Evans Douffet – dedicated to lighting up the world, not dousing it in dust! My tongue simply could not go on speaking that stuff! . . . No doubt it was excessive. I was carried – I can't deny it – further and further from the shore of fact down the slipstream of fiction. But blame the house – not the spirit which defied it!

LOTTE: And this is your defence?

LETTICE: Where people once left yawning they now leave *admiring*. I use that word in its strict old sense – meaning a State of Wonder. That is no mean defence.

LOTTE: It is completely irrelevant!

LETTICE: Last month I put out a soup bowl by the rear exit. Not from greed – though heaven knows I could be forgiven that, with what you pay me. I wanted *proof*! People express gratitude the same way all over the world: with their *money*. (*Proudly*) *My soup bowl brims!* It brims every evening with their coins, as they themselves are brimming! I watch them walking away afterwards to the car park, and those are *Brimming People*. Every one!

LOTTE: (*Tartly*) Really? If you were to look through these letters you might discover quite a few who were not actually brimming – except with indignation.

(LETTICE *approaches the desk and examines a letter.*)

LETTICE: Churls are always with us. Curmudgeons are never slow to come forward.

LOTTE: (*Furious*) *Twenty-two letters!* I have twenty-two letters about you, Miss Douffet . . . None of them exactly written in a state of wonder!

LETTICE: (*Loftily*) Twenty-two – what's *that*? . . . I have fifty – sixty! Here – look for yourself! Here! . . . Behold! . . . Here! (*She grabs her satchel and empties its contents over the desk – a small avalanche of envelopes.*)

Vox populi! The Voice of the People! . . . I wrote my address beside my soup bowl. This is the result!

LOTTE: (*Protesting*) Please, Miss Douffet! . . . This is my desk!

LETTICE: (*Hotly*) Read them. Read for yourself! . . . *There* is my defence. The Voice of the People! . . . Read!

LOTTE: (*Exploding*) *I will not! I will not!* This is nonsense – all of it! They don't matter! . . . None of this matters – your mother – your childhood – your car park – *I don't care!* (*Pause; struggling to control herself*) I am not in the entertainment business – and nor are you. That is all. We are guarding a heritage. Not running a theatre. That is all.

(*She glares at* LETTICE. *Four violent knocks are heard on the door.*)

Yes! . . . What?

(MISS FRAMER *comes in nervously, bearing a tray of tea with scones, butter and jam.*)

FRAMER: The tea, Miss Schoen.

LOTTE: (*Calmer*) Would you like some tea?

LETTICE: That would be kind.

LOTTE: As strong as you can make it for *me*, please, Miss Framer.

FRAMER: Yes, Miss Schoen.

LETTICE: (*Brightly to* FRAMER) So strong you can trot a mouse on it, my mother used to say.

FRAMER: Oh, that's good! That's very good! 'Trot a mouse'! . . . Oh! Did you hear that, Miss Schoen?

(*She and* LETTICE *laugh conspiratorially together, until* LOTTE *gives her an icy look.*)

LOTTE: Miss Framer, please.

(*The laughter dies.* LOTTE *picks up one of* LETTICE*'s envelopes. She reads the enclosed letter.*)

FRAMER: (*To* LETTICE) There's a scone and jam if you would like.

LETTICE: Have you no marmalade?

FRAMER: I'm afraid not.

LETTICE: You really should, in this office. It's a much more historical preserve. Do you not know the origin of that word?

FRAMER: Marmalade? I'm afraid not.

LETTICE: *You* know it, I'm sure, Miss Schoen.

LOTTE: What?

LETTICE: The origin of the word marmalade.

LOTTE: Regretfully, no.

(*She returns to reading the letter.*)

LETTICE: (*To* FRAMER, *undeterred*) Mary Queen of Scots. She was frequently sick with headaches–

(FRAMER *glances at* LOTTE.)

– as who could blame her, poor confined woman? Each time she fell ill she would call for a special conserve of oranges and sugar. Her maids would whisper among themselves in French, 'Bring the preserve – Marie is sick! *Marie est malade*!' . . . Do you see? *Marie est malade* – marmalade!

FRAMER: Oh yes! Too extraordinary! . . . You should perhaps take some when you have one of your heads, Miss Schoen.

LOTTE: Thank you, Miss Framer; that will be all for the present.

FRAMER: Yes, Miss Schoen.

(*She hurries from the room.*)

LETTICE: (*Drinking her tea*) Do you have headaches?

LOTTE: (*Reading*) Now and then, yes.

LETTICE: I'm sorry.

LOTTE: We all have something.

LETTICE: Your assistant could be right. Perhaps what eased Queen Mary could also help you.

LOTTE: Perhaps.

LETTICE: Which letter is that? The one that says I light up the corridors of the past as with a blazing torch?

LOTTE: No, this is the lady in the green sweater.

LETTICE: Ah yes!

LOTTE: (*Reading aloud*) 'Dear Miss, I was the lady in the green sweater last Wednesday afternoon to whom you explained the portrait of a boy wearing leaves in his hair. It was so fascinating to learn the truth about that picture. If I had not asked I would never have learnt that terrible story of the young heir murdered by his uncle with a garland of poisonous herbs. I had never realized that one could actually kill people through the scalp in that way. How clever it was of you to remind me of the extraordinary death in *Hamlet* where the old King is poisoned through his *ears*. It just goes to show that Shakespeare thought of everything first . . .'

(*A pause.* LETTICE *looks at her and smiles self-excusingly.*)

LETTICE: The Trust itself admits that boy's end was mysterious.

LOTTE: You must see yourself – it's no good, any of this. As I said, we are not running a theatre. If you were a playwright you could legitimately stand by your soup bowl and expect to see it filled for your invention. To some people – incomprehensible as it is to me – that is not only allowable but even praiseworthy. A tour guide however is not a paid fantasist, and in her such an action remains merely dishonest.

LETTICE: I cannot accept 'merely' . . . I do not do anything *merely*.

LOTTE: Untruth is untruth. It will find no endorsement in this office. Now let us not go on with this.

LETTICE: Read one more letter. The one in the blue envelope. The writer is a director of the Royal Shakespeare Company. He says adventure is in the air whenever I open my mouth.

LOTTE: That is entirely the trouble.

LETTICE: Why trouble?

LOTTE: Please! . . . This is unpleasant enough.

LETTICE: Yes! Of course! I understand! We live in a country now that *wants* only the *Mere*. Mere Guides. Mere People. Mere Events. I understand completely!

LOTTE: Miss Douffet, let me be frank. (*Pause.*) There is no possible way I can justify your continued employment with the Trust.

(*A long pause.*)

LETTICE: So. I am condemned.

LOTTE: You are found, regrettably, unsuitable.

LETTICE: When do I leave?

LOTTE: Right away, I think, would be best.

LETTICE: I could finish the summer. There's not so very much of it left.

LOTTE: On balance I would rather you didn't.

LETTICE: I see. Well. Good. Yes. Of course . . . It is really the more merciful way, I grant you that. Instant oblivion.

LOTTE: Please now, Miss Douffet!

LETTICE: No, no, you are kind in your ruthless way. You don't leave one, as some tyrants might do, to languish in the prison of false hope. Away with her to sudden and peremptory death! I thank you!

LOTTE: (*Exasperated*) Oh, for God's sake! Can't we dispense with theatrics for just one moment? You are after all only going to another job.

LETTICE: (*Suddenly crying out*) *Really?* . . . Am I? . . . And where do you imagine I shall find that – at my age?

(*A long pause.*)

LOTTE: I will try to compose a reference of some sort for you.

LETTICE: Please do not. I would not ask you to lie on my behalf.

LOTTE: I wouldn't lie, Miss Douffet. Something no doubt can be thought up.

LETTICE: That is not your forte, Miss Schoen, thinking things up. At the moment you exude a certain grey integrity. Please do not try to contaminate it with colour.

LOTTE: (*Through gritted teeth*) You are not fair. You are not fair at all. Not at all!

LETTICE: (*Rising*) I have joined the ranks of the Unemployed. Fairness is not one of our salient characteristics.

(LOTTE *presses the buzzer. We hear it.*)

I leave you with a true story concerning colour. Check it in the books, if you like, for accuracy. Are you aware how the Queen of Scots behaved at the moment of her execution?

LOTTE: Without theatrics, I hope.

LETTICE: Not at all. Quite the reverse. It was the custom for victims on the scaffold to shed their outer garments to avoid soiling them with blood.

(MISS FRAMER *comes in.* LETTICE *includes her in the story.*)

Queen Mary appeared in a dress of deepest black. But when her ladies removed this from her – what do you imagine was revealed?

LOTTE: I really can't guess.

LETTICE: (*To* MISS FRAMER) Can you?

(*The secretary shakes her head helplessly: No!* LETTICE *begins to loosen her cloak.*)

A full-length shift was seen. A garment the colour of the whoring of which she had been accused! The colour of martyrdom – and defiance! Blood red!

(*She steps out of her cloak to reveal a brilliant red nightdress to her feet, embossed all over with little golden crowns.* MISS FRAMER *gasps.*)

Yes – all gasped with the shock of it! All watched with unwilling admiration – that good old word again – all watched with *wonder* as that frail captive, crippled from her long confinement, stepped out of the darkness of her nineteen years' humiliation and walked into eternity – a totally self-justified woman! (*To* LOTTE) That is strict and absolute fact. A long goodbye to you.

(*She sweeps up her cloak from the floor and walks triumphantly out of the office.* LOTTE SCHOEN *stares after her in amazed fascination.* MISS FRAMER *stands goggling. The curtain falls.*)

ACT TWO

Lettice Douffet's basement flat in Earl's Court, London. Several weeks later.

Entry to this flat, as with many Victorian houses in London, is achievable only through the front door of the house on street level above, and thence down a staircase.

We can see this staircase, dingy and covered with linoleum, when LETTICE *opens the door to her flat. Also clearly visible is a large bay window through which can be seen a typically drab 'area'; a section of the pavement above it, with street lamp; the steps going up to the front door on one side of it; and the legs – just the legs – of anyone walking past the house or entering it. Indeed, a man walks by as the curtain rises, establishing this.*

*The room is poorly furnished, but contains several curious theatrical relics, including a sword and two thrones – one in plain wood, one gilded. On the walls is a flamboyant poster advertising 'La Compagnie Etonnante "*LES BARBARES*" Dans le Drame le Plus Horrifique de Shakespeare:* RICHARD III. *Avec la Grande Vedette Anglaise* ALICE EVANS DOUFFET *dans le Rôle Prodigieux du Roi Assassin!'*

We see three doors in all. One leads to the bedroom, one to the kitchen, and the main one, already mentioned, which opens to reveal the staircase from the ground floor. Beside this main door is an intercom telephone on the wall, connecting with the front door outside.

It is early evening. Seated in the gilded throne is LETTICE, *holding aloft a large furry cat.*

LETTICE: (*To the cat*) My name is Felina, Queen of Sorrows! I allow this handmaid to hold me so intimately only that she may admire me better. My eyes are the colour of molten topaz. Many proud Toms have drowned themselves in Old Nile for love of them! My lot is tragedy. I was cast forth from my palace beside the tumbling cataract – imprisoned cruelly in a dungeon beneath the Earl's Court Road! I, who dined off crayfish and Numidian scallops, forced to eat squalid preparations out of *tins* – the Whiskas and Munchies of Affliction!

(*The legs of* LOTTE SCHOEN *walk into view above, cross the window, and go up the steps to the front door.*)

No matter, I will endure all – and when the time is ripe, the whole world will see my triumphant restoration to the throne! Then all will perish who wounded me – their eyes scratched from their treasonous heads!

(*The buzzer of the intercom sounds loudly.* LETTICE *starts, alarmed.*)

Who's that? . . .

(*Hastily she rises and peers up cautiously at the legs on the front steps, holding the cat.*)

(*To it*) What do you think? Hard legs, yes? . . . Proud, cat-kicking legs, I'd say . . . I wouldn't trust them, would you?

(*The buzzer sounds again harshly, making her jump.*)

Oh dear . . .

(*Nervously she goes to the intercom by the door and lifts the phone.*)

(*Into it*) Yes? . . . Who is it, please?

(*We in the theatre hear what* LETTICE *hears in her receiver, through speakers.*)

LOTTE: (*Brisk*) Miss Douffet?

LETTICE: (*Faintly*) Yes . . .

LOTTE: This is Miss Schoen.

LETTICE: Who?

LOTTE: Miss Schoen. From the Trust. Do you remember?

(LETTICE *stands aghast.*)

Hallo? . . . Miss Douffet? . . . Are you there?

LETTICE: (*In a whisper*) Yes . . .

LOTTE: Can you hear me? (*Insistent*) Miss Douffet? Can you hear me?

LETTICE: (*To the cat*) It's her . . . The Executioner!

(*The buzzer sounds again, imperiously.*)

(*Into the phone; louder*) Hallo?

LOTTE: Please let me in. I have to see you.

LETTICE: No!

LOTTE: It's just for a moment. You won't regret it, I assure you.

LETTICE: (*Faintly*) I don't choose . . . I really do not.

LOTTE: What are you saying? I can't hear you!

LETTICE: (*A little louder*) I do not choose to receive you. Please go away.

LOTTE: Miss Douffet, I do very much need to see you. Please let me in. (*Pause.*) Are you listening?

(*We see* LOTTE *crouching down and peering through the side window, trying to see in. She raps sharply on the railings with her umbrella.* LETTICE *shrinks back against the wall. The face disappears, and the buzzer goes again. And again. And again.*)

(*Raising her voice; sharply*) Miss Douffet, this is absurd! Please let me in at once!

(*A long blast on the buzzer.*)

Miss Douffet, I insist!

LETTICE: (*In distress*) Oh dear . . . Very well!

(*She presses the button to release the catch on the front door, and opens the one to her flat.*)

(*Calling up the stairs*) Enter if you must! Down to the dungeon!

(LOTTE*'s legs disappear into the house.* LETTICE *stands rigid. We hear feet marching down the stairs and* LOTTE *appears.*)

LOTTE: Good afternoon. It is very good of you to see me. (*Seeing the cat in* LETTICE*'s arms*) *Ah!*

(*She retreats in panic, half closing the door.*)

LETTICE: What is it?

LOTTE: A cat!

LETTICE: This is Felina.

LOTTE: I'm sorry, I can't come in! Not with that!

LETTICE: Why not?

LOTTE: Allergy. The doctor calls it that anyway. I know it's something deeper. Either way it prevents my entering.

LETTICE: She can be banished for five minutes.

LOTTE: I'd be grateful.

LETTICE: Very well.

(LETTICE *goes into the bedroom with Felina and returns alone, shutting the door. Cautiously* LOTTE *enters the flat.*)

(*Coldly*) She is confined in the shoe cupboard.

LOTTE: Thank you. That's most kind.

LETTICE: Not to her. She prefers being in here . . . What did you mean, something deeper than allergy?

LOTTE: I have an actual aversion to cats. Their sinuousness and slyness. I try to conquer it but can't. They actually make my throat swell.

LETTICE: Well, that's mutual. Felina's throat swells when she meets *people* she doesn't like. They are creatures of deep instinct, of course.

LOTTE: So I have been told.

LETTICE: Would you like to sit down?

(*She gestures to the wooden throne.*)

LOTTE: What an interesting chair. Was it one of your mother's?

LETTICE: How do you know that?

LOTTE: It looks rather like a prop.

LETTICE: That is her Falstaff chair.

(LOTTE *looks at her, startled.*)

You may occupy it if you like. (*Indicating the gilded chair*) Or you may take the endored one.

LOTTE: I wouldn't presume.

LETTICE: You have my assent.

LOTTE: Well . . . thank you.

(*She sits on the wooden one. An awkward pause.* LETTICE *goes into the kitchen.*)

Miss Douffet, I hope my coming here is not disturbing for you.

LETTICE: Why should it be? After all, you have no powers here.

LOTTE: I beg your pardon?

(LETTICE *returns with a tin of cat food, which she opens and empties into a bowl.*)

LETTICE: You have done all you can to me. I am quite beyond your jurisdiction.

LOTTE: My dear woman, I haven't come to *do* anything to you.

LETTICE: Don't . . . don't say that, please . . . I am not 'dear' to you. I am not dear at all.

LOTTE: It was just a form of words.

LETTICE: I respect words.

LOTTE: So do I. Intensely.

LETTICE: Why have you come? To gloat? To look on my condition?

LOTTE: To see how you are, certainly.

LETTICE: Well then, you see! Behold!

LOTTE: You've been well?

LETTICE: I can't believe you're interested in that.

LOTTE: You have found some work, one hopes?

LETTICE: Does one?

LOTTE: Of course. I'm sure it's not easy.

LETTICE: Oh yes! In my case – very!

LOTTE: Really?

LETTICE: Extremely, actually. (*Cold*) Since I saw you it has been, I think, ten weeks.

LOTTE: About that, yes.

LETTICE: In that period I have worked for *one* . . . I found employment in a large store in Oxford Street. In the food department during British Cheese Week. I had to dress up in a green crinoline and a pink muslin cap – and offer samples of a new cheese called Devon Dream. My week did not run its full course.

LOTTE: You left?

LETTICE: I was asked to leave.

LOTTE: I'm sorry. May I ask why?

LETTICE: I would rather not delve into it.

(*She goes into the bedroom with the bowl of cat food. A loud miaow sends* LOTTE *in renewed panic over to the stairs.* LETTICE *comes back into the room to find her there with some surprise. She shuts the bedroom door and* LOTTE *cautiously returns to her chair.*)

LOTTE: Miss Douffet . . . to come to the point: since we met, you have been somewhat on my conscience.

LETTICE: (*Coldly*) Really?

LOTTE: I am aware it is not easy for you – for us, people of our age and background – to find employment of any kind – let alone that which suits us . . . I have been keeping an eye open on your behalf.

LETTICE: How peculiar.

LOTTE: Peculiar?

LETTICE: To push someone in the gutter and then toy with pulling them out. Remorse, my mother used to say, is a useless emotion.

LOTTE: (*Stiffly*) It is hardly that, I can assure you. I was not remotely wrong in doing what I did. I would do it again. All the same . . . in a friendly spirit – I have been on the watch for you. That is all I'm saying. If it's of interest. (*A pause.*) I have actually discovered something you might enjoy doing. Should I go on?

LETTICE: (*Equally stiffly*) If you wish.

LOTTE: A married couple who live next door to me run a business of tourist boats on the Thames. The public embark at Westminster Bridge and are addressed throughout by a guide using a microphone. I have been speaking to this couple, and they are badly in need of helpers: people who have enthusiasm for history – with particular regard to the river. I told them I knew exactly the person. I did somewhat exceed the limits of veracity – but if you were interested you could easily read up the subject – at least sufficiently not to make a liar out of me . . . You would of course have to swear to me absolutely that there would be no departures of any kind from the strictest historical truth . . . (*Pause.*) The pay is not enormous, but there are tips – this time legitimately sanctioned by the management – and these apparently can be generous. Also, of course, though I should not say it, they need not be declared . . . I have provided for you, on the notepaper of the Preservation Trust, a letter of reference, which could be useful in impressing my friends – and indeed other possible employers in the future . . . Would you care to see it?

LETTICE: If you would care to show it.

(LOTTE *takes the letter from her handbag and gives it to* LETTICE.) (*Reading it aloud*) 'This is to introduce Miss Douffet. Working as a guide for the Trust, Miss Douffet became a popular favourite with many members of the visiting public. During the last few months of her employment especially, they showed their appreciation of her particular style by writing many letters expressing gratitude. Besides an extensive knowledge of history, Miss Douffet specializes in an imaginative manner of narration essentially her own. One which ensures that any tour over which she presides becomes a veritably unforgettable experience . . .'

(*A long pause.* LETTICE *is very moved.*)

I have not deserved this.

LOTTE: Please.

LETTICE: No! Really! I have not . . . (*Increasingly upset*) I – I repaid your confidence with folly – and you reward me like this . . . It is out of all measure . . . You are – you are very good. Yes. You are a most good – a good – a very good – a good – Oh *dear*!

(*She is over the brink of tears.*)

LOTTE: (*Alarmed*) Oh, please! Please, Miss Douffet!

LETTICE: I swear – I swear to you – if I can do this job, I shall not deviate by so much as a syllable from the recorded truth! . . . I shall read and read! I shall commit to memory every recorded fact about the river! I shall not depart from them by so much as one cedilla – not a jot or tittle! Not one iota!

LOTTE: (*Embarrassed*) Please, Miss Douffet!

(LETTICE *tears the property sword off the wall and kneels, holding it up.*)

LETTICE: *I swear this!* . . . Not one complaint will you hear! Not a single – not a single – a sing–

(*Her tears overcome her again, more freely than before.* LOTTE *is horrified by the emotion shown.*)

LOTTE: Oh, please now! Please – Really, Miss Douffet! I beg you! Please! This is quite unnecessary . . . I'm only too glad to be of help! . . . *Please!* Really and truly, I can assure you – (*Wildly, as the sobs continue*) Do you possibly have a cup of tea? That would be so nice! A cup of strong hot tea . . . ?

LETTICE: (*Bewildered*) What?

LOTTE: Or coffee! Coffee would do! . . . Or Coca-Cola! I must admit to a fondness for Coca-Cola!

(LETTICE *stops sobbing and looks at her blankly.*)

LOTTE: But of course you wouldn't have that, would you?

(LETTICE *shakes her head: No.*)

Well, anything will do. A glass of plain water would be delicious!

LETTICE: (*Recovering*) No! . . . *Quaff!*

LOTTE: What?

LETTICE: Quaff! That's its name. You must have Quaff!

LOTTE: What's that?

LETTICE: Perfect . . . Just perfect for the occasion!

LOTTE: Quaff?

LETTICE: My cordial. Sixteenth century! . . . It's one of my greatest hobbies – the food and drink of Tudor times. Would you – could you possibly bear to sample it? I'd be so delighted if you could! . . . Would you let me toast you in it now?

LOTTE: (*Nervously*) I don't know . . . I drink very little.

LETTICE: Oh, yes, please! You must try it: it's very enlarging! When I am alone I do not dare to even sip it – it makes me too full of song and story! . . . Say yes – please!

LOTTE: Well – just a very little.

LETTICE: I'll get it! (*She moves excitedly towards the kitchen.*) It has stayed in the kitchen untasted for far too long . . . We'll have it in goblets! I have two splendid ones Mother used in the tavern scene in *Henry IV*! . . . Take your coat off, I entreat it.

LOTTE: Thank you.

(LETTICE *disappears.* LOTTE *removes her coat. From the kitchen we hear* LETTICE *singing 'And let me the cannikin clink, clink!' from* Othello, *in a jubilant high voice. She reappears carrying a tray with two theatrical goblets studded with fake jewels, and a bottle of gilded liquor.*)

LETTICE: Here it is . . . Pour generously!

(*She sets down the tray and proffers the goblets to* LOTTE *who picks up the bottle and pours gingerly.*)

No, no, please – more! It is not meant to drip into the glass but to *cascade*! . . . That's better. And now we *quaff.* Which being interpreted means – knock it back! (*Toasting*) To you! . . . Of course you can't drink to yourself, so I'll just do it and then you can follow: 'To Miss Schoen – a generous friend!' (*She swallows it, gasping delightedly.*)

LOTTE: Now it's my turn. 'To Miss Douffet – who surprised me greatly!'

LETTICE: Oh, that's charming!

(LOTTE *swallows her drink – and gasps also at its strength.* LETTICE *is delighted.*)

Enlarging, isn't it?

LOTTE: It certainly is . . . What on earth is in it?

LETTICE: The pleasure it offers is both herbal and verbal. That's my little riddle. (*Pause.*) I imagine I appear rather an alien person to you.

LOTTE: That is not all bad, I suspect.

LETTICE: Let us recharge.

LOTTE: Is that wise?

LETTICE: Absolutely. One is never sufficient.

LOTTE: Well, all right – if I can linger with it a little. Less quaff and more sip.

LETTICE: At your pleasure.

LOTTE: What is your first name?

LETTICE: Lettice.

LOTTE: That's pretty.

LETTICE: It comes from Laetitia – the Latin word for gladness. As a vegetable it is obviously one of God's mistakes – but as a name it passes, I think.

LOTTE: Indeed. (*Toasting*) To Lettice!

LETTICE: (*Shyly*) Thank you . . . What's yours? No – don't answer. Let me play the interviewer for once: you be the victim.

LOTTE: I don't think that's a very good idea.

LETTICE: Why not? It'll be a game! Imagine you are looking for employment and I'm the woman at the agency. In front of me is an enormous desk, covered with details of jobs – for none of which you're suitable. That's what they always imply anyway. (*Stern voice*) 'Sit down, please, Miss – er, Schoen, isn't it?'

LOTTE: Correct.

(*She sits.* LETTICE *sits too, severely. They face each other seated on the two thrones.*)

LETTICE: What is your first name?

LOTTE: Charlotte.

LETTICE: Charlotte Schoen. Hardly an English name.

LOTTE: No, my father was German.

LETTICE: But your mother was English?

LOTTE: Correct.

LETTICE: Of honest yeoman stock?

LOTTE: I don't know about that. She worked for the Home Office.

LETTICE: And your father: what was his work?

LOTTE: He published art books. The Perseus Press.

LETTICE: Oh, good heavens! He owned that?

LOTTE: You know it?

LETTICE: Very well! They are ravishing, those Perseus books! There's one in particular on the Baroque which is absolutely exquisite. It makes one almost swoon with delight.

LOTTE: That is entirely wrong, I'm afraid.

LETTICE: Is it?

LOTTE: Well, of course! Officials in employment agencies don't swoon.

LETTICE: I suppose they don't.

LOTTE: You have to show far more reserve than that.

LETTICE: How silly of me. Forgive me . . . (*The interviewer again*) What was your education, please?

LOTTE: St Paul's School for Girls. Then the Regency Street Polytechnic, for architecture.

LETTICE: You studied to be an architect?

LOTTE: Correct.

LETTICE: And qualified?

LOTTE: I'm afraid not. My mother ran off with someone in her office. After that my father became ill and needed me. The business was sold for far too little. We moved out of a large house in Kensington, into a small flat in Putney. I became more and more his nurse.

LETTICE: I'm sorry.

LOTTE: No need to be. He was worth it. He gave me a unique childhood.

LETTICE: Surrounded by art books on every civilization!

LOTTE: Yes. We had an enormous library where I virtually lived.

At one end there was a huge window of coloured glass – emerald and gold.

LETTICE: How lovely!

LOTTE: It's still there. Last week I walked by and there was a girl looking out of it with a completely shaven head, except for three spikes of green hair standing straight up like ice-cream cones.

LETTICE: Marie Antoinette would have loved that.

LOTTE: She would?

LETTICE: Oh yes! She used to wear the most elaborate styles on her own head. Great ships at anchor on a sea of tossing curls! . . . I didn't invent that.

(LOTTE *looks at her severely.*)

LOTTE: I hope you are not one of those people who see good in anything – no matter how grotesque.

LETTICE: As Christians we are surely meant to perceive good wherever we can.

LOTTE: I am not a Christian, and the only good I perceive is in beauty . . . This world gets uglier by the minute, that's all I perceive for sure. I used to love the walls of our house: that cream stucco so characteristic of London. Now they are completely defaced with slogans. One says, 'Hang the bloody Pope'. Another says, 'Hang the bloody Prots'.

LETTICE: I can't read the writing on the walls round us. It's all in Arabic.

LOTTE: I wouldn't feel too deprived. I'm sure it's only saying hang someone else.

LETTICE: I just know it's all done by Mr Pachmani.

LOTTE: Who is that?

LETTICE: My neighbour upstairs. Obviously a political conspirator . . . I just know he slinks out at night with a paintpot and brush, looking for new walls to conquer.

LOTTE: In his country they'd cut off hands for that. Perhaps we should do the same.

LETTICE: How ferocious! A totally Shakespearian punishment! Aaron the Moor wields the axe – and the defacer's hand is rendered powerless for ever! I've always thought offenders should have the word 'Vandal' sprayed on their foreheads with indelible paint – but your sentence is much more extreme!

LOTTE: This entire city is actually crammed with fanatics from all over the globe fighting medieval crusades on our ground. Isn't it time we became a little fanatic ourselves on its behalf? . . . People in the past would not have endured it. But, of course, they had spunk. There's no one left now with any spunk at all.

LETTICE: Just the Mere! . . . The Mere People! That's all who remain.

LOTTE: Ghosts! They're the worst! That's what we must never become ourselves – you and I. Not that there's much danger of it in your case.

LETTICE: Ghosts?

LOTTE: Gentlewomen who live in the past and wring their hands. My office is filled with them. Wring, wring, wring – all day long. (*Genteel voice*) 'Oh, my goodness! Oh, what have we come to? Oh, this dreadful modern age!' . . . They should all be selling fragrant cushions in our gift shops! Or Tudor House tea towels! . . . I'm taking a course at this moment. Computers – processors – the whole modern thing. (*Accusingly*) How are you on all that?

LETTICE: Not expert, I must confess. I prefer the world of the handmade. The world of Quaff and Conversation.

LOTTE: (*Who is beginning to feel its influence*) Well, I have to admit the Quaff is surprisingly good – once one gets used to it. (*She toasts* LETTICE, *who responds.*) Is it really sixteenth century? One can hardly believe it.

LETTICE: An adaptation. By me. I regard it as an *hommage*, as the French say. My bow to Tudor times.

LOTTE: And you're not saying what's in it?

LETTICE: (*Archly*) Both herbal and verbal! . . .

LOTTE: Well, one thing I can tell – it's extremely strong.

LETTICE: Naturally. Our ancestors possessed strong stomachs. Remember Falstaff! *He* wasn't Mere, was he? He was the absolute antithesis of the Mere! . . . Let's have a toast to him! My favourite character in all drama!

LOTTE: Really?

LETTICE: Certainly! The ton of man, fat as butter! Who's yours?

LOTTE: I think I told you I don't share your passion for the drama. In fact I despise it. However one does admire spunk. So – to Falstaff!

LETTICE: Falstaff! The old bed-presser!

(LOTTE *looks startled. They both drink.*)

LOTTE: Did your mother actually play that part herself?

LETTICE: Many times! He was her most successful role – after Richard III. She virtually wore the same costume for both. It was merely a matter of turning the pillow round she used as a hump, from the back to the front. (*Patting her stomach and rumbling*) 'Holla! Maîtresse Quickly! *Holla!*' . . . It was utterly convincing. I remember she had beautiful white whiskers, and her cheeks would glow like port-lamps on an ocean liner.

LOTTE: There was obviously nothing mere about her either. What was her watchword again?

LETTICE: 'Enlarge – enliven – enlighten!'

LOTTE: Splendid! . . . Here's to her! Your mother!

(*She drinks.*)

LETTICE: (*Pleased*) Thank you.

LOTTE: She's not still performing, by any chance?

LETTICE: Ah, no. She died from a heart attack six years ago – on stage, playing Marc Antony in *Julius Caesar*. She was always a thought too vigorous in the forum scene . . . Still, she went as she always wished – in harness. She used to say, 'When my time comes, I want to go in a second. None of those nasty French nursing homes for me. Three-day-old croissants and wine you can run a car on!'

LOTTE: She was quite right. The Gallic spirit thrives on parsimony.

LETTICE: Tell me, is your father departed also?

LOTTE: Oh yes.

LETTICE: I drink to him anyway! . . . I'm sure he was not one of your ghosts.

LOTTE: Well, there, alas, you are wrong, my dear. That, I am afraid, is exactly what he *was*. Or at least became . . . It was inevitable, actually. He came from Dresden as a refugee. He used to say it was the most beautiful city on earth. Then in the war the Allies burnt it to the ground defending civilization. He never got over that. He died with Europe really.

LETTICE: Europe?

LOTTE: That's the only thing that sustained him – his love for Europe. I mean the actual buildings. The towns and villages of five hundred years. All virtually destroyed in five . . . (*Pause.*) He believed anybody born after 1940 has no real idea what visual civilization means – and never can have . . . 'There used to be such a thing as the Communal Eye,' he'd say. 'It has been put out in our lifetime, Lotte – yours and mine! The disgusting world we live in now could simply not have been built when that eye was open. The planners would have been torn limb from limb – not given knighthoods!'

LETTICE: Oh, how right! How absolutely *right*! . . . I wish I'd known him!

LOTTE: Yes, well, I'm his daughter – and that's the whole trouble.

LETTICE: What do you mean?

LOTTE: Because I have his eyes. It's all he left me, and I don't want them. I wish I was blind, like everyone else.

LETTICE: Don't say that!

LOTTE: I mean it! All I am now is a freak. I have *his* disease, only worse . . . I care – I actually care more for buildings than their inhabitants. When I imagine Dresden burning, all I see are those exquisite shapes of the Baroque – domes, pediments, golden cherubs going up in flames. Not people at all, just beautiful shapes vanishing for ever . . . I'm an idolator. That's what my friend called me, and he was right . . . If I could save a great Baroque city or its people I would choose the city every time. People come again: cities never.

LETTICE: Who was that you mentioned – your friend?

LOTTE: A fellow student at the Polytechnic. Jim Mackintosh. An industrial chemist. Quite remarkably handsome.

LETTICE: (*Obligingly pouring more Quaff into Lotte's goblet*) That's exceptional, I'd say. They don't tend much to go in for beauty, do they, chemists?

LOTTE: I've never really thought about it. His hair was pure gold. When I first met him I thought he dyed it, it was so startlingly bright – but he didn't. He was known in college as the Blond Bombshell. Especially appropriate, actually.

LETTICE: What do you mean?

LOTTE: We used to walk through the city endlessly together, watching it be destroyed. That was the true Age of Destruction – the late fifties and sixties. You realize the British destroyed London ultimately, not the Germans. There would be gangs of workmen all over the place, bashing down our heritage. Whole terraces of Georgian buildings crashing to the ground. I still see those great balls of iron swinging against elegant façades – street after street! All those fanlights shattering – enchanting little doorways – perfectly proportioned windows, bash bash bash! – and no one stopping it. It was exactly like being hit oneself. One day watching, I actually threw up in the street . . . That was when I said to him, 'Do it.'

LETTICE: Do what?

LOTTE: Nothing. I'm talking too much. This stuff makes one babble.

(*She slams down her goblet.*)

LETTICE: Please don't stop. What did you mean, 'Do it'?

(*A pause.*)

LOTTE: Something I'd talked to him about before. One night standing on the South Bank outside the Shell Building . . . It was nearly finished: a great dead weight of Not Trying. Not Trying and Not Caring! I remember I was so angry looking at it, I said, 'The people who put this up should be hanged in public for debauching the public imagination!'

LETTICE: Bravo!

LOTTE: And then I said – 'Why should all the bombs just fall on beauty? Why shouldn't one at least be used on ugliness – purely as protest? Witness that someone at least still has eyes!'

LETTICE: Gracious!

LOTTE: After all, we all have to live with it. We all have to endure it for ever! Why are we all so *tame*? . . . If we really cared we would blow this up! (*More and more excited*) We would go round in secret and destroy this kind of awfulness, *all* these excrescences, anywhere we saw we had to! We'd blow these things into bits as soon as they were finished – till builders were afraid to put them up! – no, no – till architects were afraid to design them! That would make a statement in the world for all to see! . . . I said we should call ourselves the End. E.N.D. The Eyesore Negation Detachment . . .

(LETTICE *claps.*)

Jim just looked at me – his eyes were shining. He had a great deal of Scottish passion buried inside him . . . And then do you know what he said? 'A bomb is very easy to make.'

(*A long pause, during which* LETTICE *solemnly hands* LOTTE *the jug.* LOTTE *pours herself another large drink and imbibes it, deeply.*)

LETTICE: (*Breathlessly*) Go on.

LOTTE: Well, when I said, 'Do it' – he did it.

LETTICE: Made a bomb?

LOTTE: Two. One for each wing of the Shell Building. He was brilliant at science. While he was making them I was studying the site. You wouldn't believe how easy it was in the days before terrorism to get into a building still under construction. All it took was a cap and overalls – and in my case a false moustache.

LETTICE: (*Delighted*) You dressed up as a workman?

LOTTE: Exactly. I looked very convincing. Jim explained to me over and over how to activate my bomb, and then we took them in separate taxis, hidden in toolbags. I took the right wing, he took the left. It reflected our politics! . . . We decided to leave them in separate lavatories on the first floor. They were timed to explode together at four in the morning, long before anyone got to work.

(*A pause.*)

LETTICE: And?

LOTTE: (*Embarrassed*) Well . . . he put *his* into the building, and I didn't . . . I got cold feet at the last moment. Instead I dropped mine into the river, off Waterloo Bridge . . . Next morning we listened together in bed to the six o'clock news. There was nothing about any explosion. Nor on the seven, nor the eight. His obviously hadn't gone off. Now we were in the most dreadful position! Workmen were there all day long – what if it exploded when people were there? . . . He said, 'We must return at once and fetch them out!' And so then I had to confess – there was only one to fetch. He didn't say anything. Just went straight out and collected it – and brought it back home. He dismantled it in front of me on the kitchen table, in dead silence . . . That wasn't all he dismantled.

LETTICE: What do you mean?

LOTTE: Well, *Us*, of course. He dismantled us as well. He looked at me with total contempt. As if I'd betrayed him. Which of course I had.

LETTICE: No!

LOTTE: Absolutely! I'd proposed the whole thing, then run out on him behind his back. If anything had gone wrong he would have had to take the whole blame . . . We split up within days after that.

LETTICE: I'm so sorry.

LOTTE: (*Protesting*) I was *frightened* . . . I didn't want to get caught!

LETTICE: Of course not! That's understandable . . . He should have understood that!

LOTTE: (*Harshly*) Nonsense! Why should he? It was cowardly, and deserved entirely what it got . . . Entirely.

(*A pause.* LOTTE *glares.*)

LETTICE: Where is he now? Do you ever . . . see him?

LOTTE: He found a job abroad. Ironically enough with the Shell Company. A thorough waste, I thought. He was too original for that. (*Pause.*) We both wasted ourselves in the end.

LETTICE: That's not true.

LOTTE: Absolutely.

LETTICE: Why? You have a wonderful job! Everything you could wish for! . . . I know you could have been an architect – but that was just unlucky. Your father needing you, and having to give up your studies.

LOTTE: (*Stiffly*) That was not the reason. I lost interest after Jim left – and failed my exams.

LETTICE: Oh dear.

LOTTE: One deserves everything one gets in this world. In my case, the desk.

LETTICE: Desk?

LOTTE: Where I sit now. Among the ghosts . . . The Non-doer's Desk.

LETTICE: That's not fair. You do things!

LOTTE: Hire and fire. How courageous.

LETTICE: You are very hard on yourself.

LOTTE: (*Tartly*) Oh, stop it! There's no point babbling on about it. I can't imagine why I started. It was all a long time ago, and disgraceful then!

LETTICE: No!

LOTTE: Stupid, dangerous and childish. If I hadn't been driven into indiscretion by this brew of yours, I would never have told you.

(*She glares at her. A pause.*)

LETTICE: I'm glad you did.

LOTTE: Well . . . I really must go now. (*Gathering up her things*) I wish you luck with the tour boat – and if there's anything you want, don't hesitate to telephone. (*She sways dizzily.*) Oh, good gracious!

LETTICE: What's the matter?

LOTTE: Nothing. I'm fine.

LETTICE: Is it one of your headaches?

LOTTE: No. It's one too many of your drinks!

LETTICE: Oh, dear!

LOTTE: Don't worry. I'll be perfectly all right once I've had some food.

LETTICE: Let me get you some. I could make you a tansy in no time at all. That's a medieval omelette.

LOTTE: Oh, no, really! (*She produces her bottle of cologne, shakes some on to her handkerchief and applies it to her temples.*) Just tell me what on earth you put in that drink – and without the riddle, please.

LETTICE: It's nothing dangerous, I assure you. Just mead, vodka, sugar and lovage.

LOTTE: Lovage? What's that?

LETTICE: Lovage. A herb. Its name derives from 'love' and 'ache'. Ache is the medieval word for parsley.

LOTTE: You really are a unique person, Lettice. If I were you, I'd bottle it and sell it in one of those gourmet shops. You could have your own little stall.

LETTICE: Just so long as I don't have to wear a crinoline and a muslin cap.

LOTTE: Tell me – what exactly did you do in that shop in Oxford Street to get you fired? When you had to sell that British cheese?

LETTICE: Devon Dream. Well, it was absolutely vile. Have you ever eaten it? It's bright tangerine and tastes of saddle soap. I told the public not to waste its money. I said, 'You can make a far better cheese than this at home.' Then I gave them a superb recipe from the year 1600 involving rennet and rosewater. They were all delighted – except the manager, who told me to get out. The man is an absolute churl *de luxe*. (*A pause.* LOTTE *looks at* LETTICE.)

LOTTE: Would you do me a favour? Would you dine with me? I'm a member of the Palladian Club. It's for professional people associated with architecture. The food you will find extremely mere, but it has the advantage of being close by, in Holland Park.

LETTICE: (*Overwhelmed*) Well, really – I don't know what to say. That is most kind, most kind indeed . . . if you mean it.

LOTTE: I don't say what I don't mean.

LETTICE: I – haven't got a really appropriate dress.

LOTTE: There isn't such a thing in this case.

LETTICE: I could wear my cloak over this. It's decent black, as they say.

LOTTE: Your Mary Queen of Scots cloak?

LETTICE: Yes.

LOTTE: I must say as long as I live I shall not forget that moment in my office. Did you make that garment yourself?

LETTICE: Yes – for my mother. It was Lady Macbeth's nightdress.

LOTTE: To be truthful, it was really what made me come here today.

LETTICE: The nightdress?

LOTTE: The uniqueness . . . After you left I looked up the story you told about the Queen. It was every word true.

(*A pause.*)

LETTICE: Did you doubt it?

LOTTE: Well, you *have* been known to improve on history.

LETTICE: I told you – only when it needs it. That story doesn't. It's perfect. Do you know how it ended?

LOTTE: With her death, I presume.

LETTICE: Not at all. There was more. She had the very last laugh! (*Gleefully*) It was the custom after decapitating someone for the executioner to hold up the severed head to the crowd and say, 'So perish all the Queen's enemies!' Mary anticipated that – just as with the dress. She had put on for the occasion a wig of auburn hair. No one had seen her for years, so most of the onlookers didn't know it was not her own. When the headsman stooped to pick up the head, he was left clutching a handful of beautiful fair curls! The head just stayed where it was on the ground – displaying to all what she had suffered during those endless years of captivity. A skull of little cropped grey hairs . . . That is the true end of the scene, and certainly does not need improvement.

LOTTE: Absolutely not.

LETTICE: Excuse me. I'll get my cloak.

(*She goes into the bedroom.* LOTTE *is left alone, looking wonderingly after her. A pause. She goes to the table, picks up her goblet and drains it – then unexpectedly picks up the other one and drains that too to give her courage. Finally she walks around to the far side of the gilded chair and suddenly – inexplicably – drops to her knees by the golden throne, facing out front.* LETTICE *returns, wearing her black cloak, to find* LOTTE *in this position.*)

(*Alarmed*) Oh dear! What is it? Are you ill? . . . You're ill, aren't you? – and it's my fault! Oh dear, dear, dear – I've made you ill!

LOTTE: (*Calmly*) Come here.

LETTICE: I'm sorry.

LOTTE: Come here.

(*Hesitantly* LETTICE *approaches the kneeling figure.*)

Now pull . . . (*She lowers her head.*) Don't be shy: just pull.

(*Tentatively* LETTICE *extends her hand to* LOTTE*'s head.*)

Go on. Be brave.

(LETTICE *touches* LOTTE*'s hair and then pulls it. It comes away in her hand: it is a wig. Beneath it is revealed a head of fluffy grey hair.*)

(*Shyly*) So perish all the Queen's enemies!

(*A pause.* LETTICE *is overcome with amazement. She holds up the wig in delight.*)

LETTICE: Oh wonderful, wonderful! *Wonderful – beyond measure!*

(*A pause.*)

Please – have dinner just like that.

LOTTE: (*Shy*) Really?

LETTICE: Oh *yes*! . . . I never saw anything that needed improving less! . . . Honestly.

(LOTTE *takes her hand and rises.*)

LOTTE: Very well . . . I will.

(*They look at each other. Then* LETTICE *laughs: a clear bright laugh of perception, and walks away across the room. She laughs again.*)

What is it? What are you thinking?

(*But instead of replying,* LETTICE *takes off her black cloak and lays it ceremoniously at the base of the staircase, in the manner of Sir Walter Raleigh assisting Queen Elizabeth.*)

LETTICE: Come, madam. Your hedgehogs await!

(*Sumptuous music sounds.* LOTTE, *entranced, walks with an attempt at grandeur across the room, over the cloak, and up the stairs. The curtain falls.*)

ACT THREE

Lettice's flat. Six months later. Afternoon.

The room is in some disarray. The front door has clearly been smashed in, and hangs precariously against the wall, exposing the dingy staircase outside, descending from the hall above. The bedroom door is closed. One new object is a large square shape covered with a black shawl.

In the Falstaff chair, sitting quite inappropriately, is MR BARDOLPH, *a solicitor. He is in middle age, dry and professional.* LETTICE *stands looking up out of the window. There is a silence between them, which has obviously been of some duration. Outside a neighbouring clock strikes four.*

BARDOLPH: I am waiting, Miss Douffet. I hope patiently. My patience, however, is not inexhaustible. Nor is my time. I ask you again, will you now speak to me? Plainly and clearly? . . . Well?

LETTICE: (*Turning*) I really don't think you should have come here, Mr Bardolph.

BARDOLPH: I would much have preferred to interview you at my office. I did suggest that, if you recall.

LETTICE: I really feel I have a right to my privacy; criminal though it may be, in the eyes of the police. I had always assumed that being granted bail meant also being granted that. Evidently I was wrong.

BARDOLPH: My dear Miss Douffet, how can I possibly make you understand – ?

LETTICE: *Please!* Do not use that form of words to me. I am not your 'dear'. We have only met once before, please to remember.

BARDOLPH: I am fully aware of it – and a most unsatisfactory meeting it was. You told me nothing whatever.

LETTICE: I seem to recall you counselled silence.

BARDOLPH: To the police. Not to me! I am – at least I am under the impression that I am – representing you. *Defending* you, Miss Douffet. Is that remotely clear?

LETTICE: My defence will come from other quarters.

BARDOLPH: You mean you have engaged another solicitor behind my back?

LETTICE: No.

BARDOLPH: Then from whom will it come? From what other quarters?

LETTICE: I would prefer to remain silent.

BARDOLPH: This is unbelievable. Do you actually realize the situation you are in? You are charged by the police with a peculiarly unpleasant crime. You go to trial in less than five weeks, and you tell me nothing with which one can possibly defend you . . . I have nothing to go on – nothing to send to counsel! It is actually impossible for a solicitor to act for a client under such conditions!

LETTICE: Please do not distress yourself, Mr Bardolph. All will be made plain at the proper time.

BARDOLPH: By whom? When and where made plain?

LETTICE: In court. In the dock. By Miss Schoen.

BARDOLPH: *Miss Schoen?!*

LETTICE: She is, as the Bible says, my shield and my buckler.

BARDOLPH: I don't actually believe I'm hearing *any* of this . . . She is *what*??

LETTICE: My defence, in whom I rest. Is that such an obscure word for a lawyer to understand – defence?

BARDOLPH: (*Controlling himself*) Miss Douffet: it may have escaped your notice that the lady you mention is not appearing in your defence. She is a prosecution witness – *against* you. In fact she is the main witness against you.

LETTICE: (*Loftily*) That is impossible. She will speak and all will be clarified.

BARDOLPH: But she has already spoken. The police interviewed her in hospital, and it is obviously on her statement alone that there is a case to answer. We are dealing with an extremely grave offence. You are charged with attempted murder. It is somewhat unlikely that your victim will speak in your defence: victims on the whole do not tend to do that . . . Now I would much appreciate it if you would speak yourself. Forthwith!

(*A pause.*)

LETTICE: What exactly did she say? I demand to know what she said against me!

BARDOLPH: That you struck her with an axe.

LETTICE: And nothing else?

BARDOLPH: She was not in a condition to make a speech – but that really is quite sufficient for the police.

LETTICE: She said I assaulted her?

BARDOLPH: Apparently, yes.

LETTICE: And nothing else?

BARDOLPH: As far as I know.

(*A pause.*)

LETTICE: (*In sudden distress*) I have been betrayed . . . Utterly betrayed! History repeats itself for ever!

BARDOLPH: What are you saying?

LETTICE: Nothing! . . . I cannot believe it! She would never do this to me! She is the soul of honesty. Honesty and accuracy are her watchwords!

BARDOLPH: All I know is that they have brought a case on her assertion – and you have to answer it.

LETTICE: I left a message on her telephone answering machine. I said you would be coming here. I am not adept at such devices, but she will understand it all the same. She will come here herself and explain everything – you'll see. She'll come to my rescue! She'll throw the accusation back at you as deep as to the lungs!

(BARDOLPH *stands up.*)

BARDOLPH: (*Losing his patience*) Miss Douffet – I am *making* no accusation of *her*! It is *you* who are the accused – and you stand in peril of going to prison for a considerable time if you don't let me help you! Now – *for the last time* – will you speak to me or not? Otherwise I will recommend another solicitor and leave you.

(*A pause.*)

LETTICE: If she has borne false witness and delivered me into the hands of gaolers – then so be it.

BARDOLPH: That means yes? (*Pause.*) That means yes, Miss Douffet?

LETTICE: (*Exploding*) *Yes!* . . . YES!

BARDOLPH: Good.

LETTICE: I have deserved better of her. I truly have . . . (*Defiant*) Ask your questions, Mr Bardolph! I will speak everything.

BARDOLPH: Thank you . . . I will recapitulate the facts and you will correct me wherever necessary. I shall record our conversation, if you don't mind.

(*He produces a tape machine from his briefcase.* LETTICE *sits in the gilded chair.*)

LETTICE: Must you?

BARDOLPH: It makes for accuracy.

LETTICE: As you will.

BARDOLPH: Turn it on yourself, when you are ready.

(*He places it on the table beside her. But* LETTICE *has no idea how to turn it on. She makes a stab at it, but fails – pressing the eject button instead, so that the little door opens. With weary patience* BARDOLPH *closes it and starts it for her.*)

There. (*He sits.*) Now: you are Lettice Douffet?

LETTICE: (*Putting her mouth very close to the machine*) Correct.

BARDOLPH: On Wednesday the thirty-first of January this year, Constable Harris, attached to the Earl's Court Road police station –

LETTICE: The thirtieth.

BARDOLPH: I'm sorry?

LETTICE:The thirtieth of January. That's most important.

BARDOLPH: On the thirty-first of January, Constable Harris was passing outside this house: number 19 Rastridge Road. He heard a cry, which made him look down into the basement area through your window. *That* window, I take it.

LETTICE: Correct.

BARDOLPH: He saw two figures – subsequently identified as

yourself and Miss Charlotte Schoen. Miss Schoen was lying on the floor with blood pouring out of a deep cut in her head. You were standing over her, holding an axe.

LETTICE: Correct.

BARDOLPH: The constable ran up the steps and rang your bell. But you did not admit him.

LETTICE: Correct.

BARDOLPH: He rang all the bells in the house until admitted by the tenant of the flat immediately above here. A Mr Pachmeen –

LETTICE: (*Venomously*) Pachmani.

BARDOLPH: The constable then rushed downstairs and banged violently on your door, but no one answered. Finally he had to break down the door.

LETTICE: As you see. Since I lack the money to repair it, I am now at the total mercy of every marauder in London. Including Mr Pachmani, who is unquestionably violent, and almost certainly making plans upstairs at this very minute to overthrow several governments.

BARDOLPH: Just keep to the facts, please. What happened next?

LETTICE: The policeman crashed into my room.

BARDOLPH: And arrested you?

LETTICE: Yes.

BARDOLPH: Go on.

LETTICE: He called an ambulance for Lotte on Mr Pachmani's telephone, then apparently summoned help. Obviously, he found himself unable to deal with me alone. I am so formidable, you see. Two more policemen arrived almost immediately and pinioned me.

BARDOLPH: Pinioned?

LETTICE: Each grasped an arm and both led me into a waiting car. It was deeply humiliating.

BARDOLPH: You were taken to a police station?

LETTICE: And hurled into a cell.

BARDOLPH: *Hurled?*

LETTICE: Led – with brusqueness.

BARDOLPH: And then?

LETTICE: I was shown a list of solicitors whom I could consult.

BARDOLPH: For legal aid?

LETTICE: Not having a disposable income of more than fifty pounds a week, I apparently qualify for free help.

BARDOLPH: And what made you choose me?

LETTICE: Your name. Bardolph. The merry companion to Falstaff. (*Pause.*) Names can be misleading . . . The rest I think you know.

BARDOLPH: You were taken to a magistrates' court next day, and later released on bail when it was understood that the victim was not dangerously hurt . . . Now, Miss Douffet: we come to the difficult bit. Apparently Mr Pachmani told the police that violent noises frequently emanated from this flat. He is no doubt prepared to swear to this in the witness box.

LETTICE: (*Scornfully*) What sort of noises does he say – *emanated*?

BARDOLPH: Cries. Bumps. Voices raised in fury, and sometimes apparently in screaming and pleading. He is emphatic about this. He says such quarrels were a constant accompaniment to his evenings.

LETTICE: With his ears pressed to the floorboards, no doubt.

BARDOLPH: (*Testily*) I do not know the position of his ears. I do know that he has said he would rather forfeit his chance of Paradise than spend another winter living – as he put it – above those two demented female infidels.

LETTICE: (*Rising, outraged*) He says what?! The smirking, sneering Ottomite!

BARDOLPH: And that he will bear witness in the Crown Court that you and Miss Schoen fought continually, with violence. Now – is this true?

(*A pause.*)

LETTICE: Yes. In a way.

BARDOLPH: In what way? . . . Miss Douffet, please go on. I have to know what happened in this room.

(*A long pause.*)

LETTICE: Executions.

BARDOLPH: I beg your pardon?

LETTICE: Executions.

(*A pause.*)

BARDOLPH: Could you elaborate?

(*Another long pause. Then* LETTICE *speaks.* BARDOLPH *sits, riveted.*)

LETTICE: Miss Schoen and I became acquainted six months ago when I was toiling as a tour guide in Wiltshire. She was instrumental in getting me promotion to more exacting work on a river boat – for which I was rewarded with thunderous applause every time we docked at Westminster Bridge. Applause, I may say, equally for my vigour of style and historical veracity . . . Our friendship flowered beyond the summer, when, of course, the work terminated. It transpired that we both harbour an enthusiasm for the heroic figures of the Past. People of spunk, as she would say. Especially those whose distinction earned them death at the hands of the Mere. I have always been fascinated by the way such people met their ends: the pride and grandeur of the world now gone . . . As we got to know each other better, we came more and more to sit upon the ground, as Shakespeare has it, and tell sad stories of the deaths of kings. Not just kings, of course: men and women of all conditions with regal hearts . . . In the end – entirely at my instigation, I don't deny it – we (*Pause*) – we came not only to tell the sad stories but to represent them.

BARDOLPH: (*Puzzled*) Represent?

LETTICE: Recall in Show how a few monumental spirits turned History into Legend . . . The fact our country no longer produces such moments is, in our view, its gravest indictment. Laughable to you, no doubt, Mr Bardolph. But then lawyers and legends have little in common.

(BARDOLPH *stares at her, beginning to be helplessly fascinated.*)

Miss Schoen herself had to be vigorously persuaded, I admit it freely. She loathed the theatrical in all forms – at least, so she protested. However, I soon perceived she protested altogether too much. In this room I watched her perform one small but thrilling act which could have only been ventured by someone longing in her heart to do what her tongue denounced . . . In an equally small way I was able to gratify that longing.

(*A pause.*)

BARDOLPH: Let me get this absolutely clear, please. Are you saying that you persuaded Miss Schoen to act out with you the deaths of famous women from the past?

LETTICE: Not just their deaths: that would make for a very short evening. Their trials as well. And not just women – there are simply not enough of them. We would choose a different subject each week – Mary Queen of Scots – Sir Walter Raleigh – King Charles I. We would read up separately everything we could about their last days – and then together explore their fate on Friday nights. She would come here or I would go to her: she has a flat in Putney, entirely lined with books of the Perseus Press . . . What was delightful was to see her change while playing – from embarrassment to excitement . . . Of course she is not an actress: she would be the first to agree with that. I myself inherited acting blood from my mother: Miss Schoen inherited more Civil Service blood from hers. Her parts tended therefore to be mainly those of Inquisitors. But presently she began to take crowd parts as well: people who called out abuse at the scaffold. And of course she would also play all the Executioners – swinging the axe, working the guillotine and so forth.

BARDOLPH: (*Startled*) Guillotine?

LETTICE: Oh yes. We didn't just keep to the confines of Britain. I have extensive connections with France. Miss Schoen disapproved of that country, but I managed to persuade her that French heroines tend to display more spectacular aspects of spunk than British. Marie Antoinette, for example, at bay before her judges.

BARDOLPH: May I ask how exactly you managed for a guillotine?

LETTICE: A simple blackboard on an easel. You just pull out the pegs and down it comes. You have to get out of the way in time, of course.

BARDOLPH: Somewhat dangerous, I would say.

LETTICE: Without danger, Mr Bardolph, there is no theatre!

BARDOLPH: Did you dress up for these evenings?

LETTICE: Of course. For Marie Antoinette I had an excellent costume already from a former job connected with dairy produce: a green crinoline and a pink muslin cap. The cap in particular is an excellent touch. It gives me a striking resemblance to that wonderful sketch made by David as she was trundled by him on her way to execution. Do you know it?

BARDOLPH: I'm afraid not.

(MISS SCHOEN'*s legs are seen to march across the window and up the steps. She lets herself in the front door: the legs disappear.*)

LETTICE: It makes a most moving impression when I wear it in the court – standing in the prisoner's dock, one strand of hair escaping from it! Hair, of course, which used to be dressed in the most elaborate styles in all Europe . . . That was her finest hour, poor Queen, her ordeal in court. Did you know she was accused of unnatural sexual practice?

BARDOLPH: I certainly didn't.

LETTICE: Oh yes. Miss Schoen is dazzling as the Prosecutor levelling that charge. She fairly spits it at me! – 'Citizeness!' she snarls: 'Citizeness! Do you deny that in your insatiable search for sensation you even enjoyed relations with your own *son*?'

(LOTTE'*s legs are seen descending the staircase at the back. We see her head – elaborately bandaged. She comes through the broken door unobserved – slipping the keys of the flat into her bag – and stands listening behind* LETTICE, *growing increasingly angry.*)

(*Acting it for the hypnotized* BARDOLPH) I stand as one numb! A hiss of horror fills the courtroom! Then slowly – very slowly – I raise my head higher and higher up to the gallery, crammed with the vilest creatures in all Paris. 'I appeal,' I say – my voice faltering, but clearly audible – 'I appeal to every mother in this room! Do I need to answer such abomination?' . . . All stare down in wonder. Few can forbear to weep. Tears are seen, trickling down the leathern cheeks of fishwives! . . . I can tell you Lotte is absolutely glorious as an awestruck fishwife.

LOTTE: (*In a voice of thunder*) *Lettice!*

(LETTICE *jumps, badly startled. She turns and sees the outraged and bandaged woman in the wrecked doorway.*)

LETTICE: Lotte!

LOTTE: (*To* BARDOLPH) Turn that off, please!

BARDOLPH: I'm sorry?

LOTTE: *Off!* . . . Your machine. If you please.

BARDOLPH: You are Miss Schoen, I take it.

LOTTE: (*Raging*) Turn that damn thing off!

(LOTTE *advances, glaring, into the room and turns it off.*)

Now: you will ignore every word this woman has spoken.

BARDOLPH: What?

LOTTE: Every word.

BARDOLPH: I'm afraid I can't do that. She is making a statement to me. I am her solicitor.

LOTTE: Rubbish! Miss Douffet is a compulsive storyteller. I am surprised you haven't gathered that by now.

LETTICE: (*Protesting*) Lotte!

BARDOLPH: Do you mean she is lying?

LOTTE: I mean she is a romancer. Her word may not be relied on.

LETTICE: That's not true! How can you say that? Every word of that is fact! Every single word!

BARDOLPH: If you will excuse me, madam, this meeting is solely between me and my client. Your presence is quite improper.

LOTTE: This woman has been dismissed repeatedly from jobs for fabrication. I can produce countless witnesses to prove it!

LETTICE: Lotte!

LOTTE: If you bring one word of this into court I will summon people who will bear this out absolutely! Members of the Preservation Trust! Elizabethan scholars! Shop managers in Oxford Street! . . . I advise you to delete every word of that tape and find some better defence for this lady.

(*A pause. She produces her cologne and handkerchief and applies it grimly.*)

LETTICE: It's true, then.

LOTTE: What?

LETTICE: You accused me. You told the police I assaulted you . . . Answer, please.

LOTTE: I don't know.

LETTICE: What do you mean?

(LOTTE *does not reply.*)

What do you mean you don't know? (*Urgently*) *Answer me!*

LOTTE: (*Uncomfortably*) They came to me in hospital. I was doped from medicine. I had the most terrible pain in my head. You know what my heads are like at the best of times – without this!

LETTICE: (*Desperate*) *What did you say to them?*

LOTTE: *I can't remember!* They were only there a moment. One of the officers said to me, 'You've been hit by your friend with an axe: is that right?' I suppose I said yes . . . Well, it was the truth.

LETTICE: But not attacked! You weren't *attacked*!

LOTTE: I didn't say I was.

LETTICE: They assumed you *did*! That's how it must have sounded!

LOTTE: (*Petulant*) I was weak! I was so weak, and my head was splitting . . . I didn't realize what I was implying!

LETTICE: (*Crying out*) And for that I am being *tried*! . . . I'm going to be tried – in reality . . . In a *real court*!

(*A pause.*)

LOTTE: I know.

LETTICE: So then I must tell the truth. I have to explain.

LOTTE: No!

LETTICE: I have to tell them how it happened. To put things right.

LOTTE: Not with that (*the tape*). You can't use that.

LETTICE: Why not?

LOTTE: You just can't. I forbid it.

LETTICE: Well, what am I to do? Go to prison?

LOTTE: That won't happen.

LETTICE: Of course it will. Attempted murder!

LOTTE: Nonsense.

LETTICE: That's the charge!

BARDOLPH: (*Tentatively*) Excuse me –

LOTTE: There's always a way. We'll think of something.

LETTICE: What way? I am charged, Lotte! What else can I say?

LOTTE: *Invent* something, for heaven's sake! You've never been slow at it before!

BARDOLPH: (*Bolder*) Excuse me –

LETTICE: (*Joyfully*) At least – at least you didn't betray me! That's all that really matters.

LOTTE: What?

LETTICE: I thought the most dreadful things about you. I'm sorry, but it looked so bad.

LOTTE: What do you mean?

LETTICE: I thought you'd denounced me. That you told them I did it on purpose.

LOTTE: Why on earth should I say that?

BARDOLPH: (*Overbearing them*) *Excuse me!*

LOTTE: (*Rounding on him sharply*) *Yes! – What?*

BARDOLPH: Am I to understand that in your view Miss Douffet is innocent of this charge?

LOTTE: Of course she is!

BARDOLPH: And everything I have heard so far on this tape about playing games of execution is in fact true?

(*A pause.*)

Please reply.

LOTTE: Yes . . . (*Pause.*) All the same, it must not be used.

BARDOLPH: I'm afraid it may have to be. If your wound was received in the course of one of these games, it would obviously be highly relevant.

LOTTE: Don't you utter another word, Lettice! Not one more syllable – do you understand me?

BARDOLPH: Miss Schoen, please – let me continue with my questions. Miss Douffet, you are in the middle of a statement to your legal representative. If you wish to avoid extremely unpleasant consequences I suggest you continue with it *now* . . . (*Pleading*) I have to hear the end of your story before I can advise you what to do.

(*A longer pause.*)

LETTICE: Yes. I shall continue.

BARDOLPH: Most wise.

(*He presses the tape button.*)

LETTICE: I'm sorry, Lotte.

BARDOLPH: You do not have to remain if you don't wish, Miss Schoen.

(LOTTE *ignores him and sits down firmly in the Falstaff chair.*)

LETTICE: (*Desperately, to her*) What else can I *do*?

(LOTTE *ignores her too, staring straight ahead.*)

BARDOLPH: One thing has been puzzling me since you began to speak. You say this lady has always played the role of executioner and you of victim.

LETTICE: Correct!

BARDOLPH: Then in fact it would surely be she who would be holding any axe – not you.
(*A pause.*)

LETTICE: We swapped.

BARDOLPH: I'm sorry?

LETTICE: We exchanged roles. It was a wonderful moment, if I may say so . . . Lotte – Miss Schoen – elected herself to play the victim. She suggested it, not I. She came over to me as usual –

BARDOLPH: This was the day of the accident?

LETTICE: Yes. January the thirtieth. The anniversary of the execution of Charles I in 1649. Charles the Martyr. She said to me – and it must have cost her a great effort – '*I* want to play the King tonight! I'm tired of headsmen and prosecutors!' I was so happy. It represented – so much! . . . (*To* LOTTE) I'm sorry, but it did. It was wonderful when you asked.
(LOTTE *turns her head away.*)
(*To* BARDOLPH) Of course I said, 'Yes, yes – of course: *do it!* It's perfect for you, that part!' And it was! It absolutely was! She was truly glorious in it! (*To him*) I'd always played the role before, but nowhere near so well as she did it that night! . . . Her dignity in the trial was perfection. 'I deny your right,' she said – just like that: so proud and clear. 'I deny with all my breath and being your right to judge me! I will enter the shining portal of Heaven with only this on my lips.' It was sublime.

LOTTE: (*Cold and removed*) I didn't actually say any of that.

LETTICE: You did.

LOTTE: Not remotely.

LETTICE: You did, Lotte. I can hear it now.

LOTTE: Rubbish! You're 'improving' – as usual. There was no 'breath and being' and no 'portal of Heaven', shining or otherwise. That is typical *you*.

LETTICE: Well, what *did* you say?

LOTTE: I'm sure your solicitor does not need the exact wording. Continue if you must, and leave me out of it.

LETTICE: (*Stubbornly*) Not until I have heard what you actually said.

LOTTE: Oh, for God's sake! What *anyone* would say playing that part! What Charles actually did say, of course. (*Brisk*) 'I would know by what authority I am brought here. The Commons of England was never a judicial court. I would first know when it came to be so.' Plain and simple, and very intelligent. A rarity around here.

LETTICE: I sit corrected.

BARDOLPH: Please go on.

LETTICE: Well . . . she rose finally, and I must say I could not have imagined a better rise from a throne. She stood with all the passion of the Stuarts surging through her – passion such as we have never witnessed in any monarch since! Rise, Lotte – show him. I dare you to do it again!

(LOTTE *folds her arms intransigently.*)

You *are* difficult, really . . . The point was, in a masterly transition she actually *became* the King, walking to his martyrdom! I've never seen anything better done. First she asked for one of my blouses and put it over her own – to represent the two shirts he wore against the cold. A clever touch, don't you think?

BARDOLPH: (*Getting caught up*) Most imaginative, certainly.

LETTICE: And then she embarked on the last solemn journey across St James's Park to the balcony at Whitehall – and made it *unforgettable*! She simply walked – (*Pause.*) I don't know how she did it, but she simply walked round this room, her head erect, and I saw it all. The freezing sunless morning – the company of nervous infantry – the slim, bearded man all in black, walking steadfastly over the frosty grass towards his death. Muffled drums sounded all the way – that was my part, of course, the muffled drums – big ones and little ones both beating out the knell of the last true monarch. Pam-tititi-pam! . . . Pam-tititi-pam! . . . Pam-tititi-pam! . . . Pam-tititi-pam! . . . (*To* LOTTE) Won't you help me? Show him what you did?

(LOTTE *turns grimly away from her.*)

All right, I'll do it alone. It won't be as good, but I'll show him.

LOTTE: (*Low*) Don't be stupid.

LETTICE: I will. (*Miming the drums*) Pam-tititi-pam! . . . Pam-tititi-pam!

LOTTE: (*Through gritted teeth*) Lettice – stop it now!

(LETTICE *starts to march around the room, playing her invisible drum.*)

LETTICE: Pam-tititi-pam! . . . Pam-tititi-pam! . . . All the drums of London beating out together! (*Louder*) *Pam-tititi-pam! Pam-tititi-pam! Pam-tititi-pam! Pam-tititi-pam!*

LOTTE: (*Exploding over this*) Lettice! Stop this at *once*! You are making a complete fool of yourself! This has nothing whatever to do with anything!

BARDOLPH: Excuse me, but I think it has, Miss Schoen. I would very much like to see what occurred next.

LETTICE: (*Defiantly*) And so you shall! We came to the block: that's what happened next. The dread block of execution!

BARDOLPH: What did you actually use for that? That stool perhaps?

LETTICE: (*Loftily*) Certainly not. We're not amateurs. We can do better than that, I hope . . . Behold! *Voilà!*

(*She whisks the black shawl off the big shape to reveal an executioner's block.*)

BARDOLPH: (*Impressed*) Where on earth did you find that?

LETTICE: (*Secretively*) Ah-ha!

BARDOLPH: It's not real? It can't possibly be real! . . . Is it?

LETTICE: What do *you* think?

BARDOLPH: I don't know . . . Tell me.

LETTICE: Guess. What would you say?

(*A pause. He examines it.*)

BARDOLPH: I'm not sure . . . I can't tell . . . Yes!

(LETTICE *laughs delightedly.*)

LETTICE: Ah-ha! Fooled you!

BARDOLPH: It *isn't*?

LETTICE: No! But it looks perfect, doesn't it? Isn't it absolutely perfect?

BARDOLPH: I'd never have known!

LETTICE: No one would! We looked for a real one, of course. (*To* LOTTE) We actually looked for ages, didn't we? We searched all the antique shops in London, just about. The Portobello Road – Islington Market – everywhere. There wasn't one to be found . . . I scoured the catalogues of Sotheby's and Christie's: one never seemed to come up. Thumbscrews now and then, and once an Iron Maiden of Nuremberg – but never a block. Don't you think that's odd?

BARDOLPH: Well, yes – now you come to mention it. I mean, there must have been blocks all over England at one time.

LETTICE: Exactly. As you can imagine we were in despair, because we needed one desperately. Until she had her inspiration. Tell him, Lotte.

(*Pause.*)

BARDOLPH: (*To* LOTTE) Please . . . I'm most interested. How did you solve the problem?

LOTTE: (*Grimly*) I used my brains. If one wishes to find a block, where does one go?

BARDOLPH: I really can't think: where?

LOTTE: To a forest, naturally.

BARDOLPH: So where did you go?

LETTICE: Epping. It's not far by bus. She was quite right – there were hundreds of suitable logs strewn about. It was just a question of shaping one.

BARDOLPH: (*Now deeply involved*) But how did you get it home? By taxi?

LOTTE: Of course not. Do you imagine we can afford taxis from Epping Forest to Earl's Court? We took the bus. The driver was most uncooperative.

LETTICE: He said he wasn't paid to carry lumber.

LOTTE: Pedantic man.

LETTICE: But she was brilliant! She said, 'We are fungus experts from the Ministry of Health. We have found a very rare variety of fungus growing on this log. It could prove of the utmost benefit to medical research.'

BARDOLPH: Most inspired.

LOTTE: (*Coldly*) Thank you.

BARDOLPH: So now we come to the execution. I presume that is where the accident occurred.

LETTICE: Oh yes: I'm afraid so.

BARDOLPH: Please show me in detail, if you can.

LETTICE: That's easy. Lotte, you've got to do this. It's evidence.

LOTTE: Just describe it, Lettice. It doesn't need illustration.

BARDOLPH: I would rather it had it, if you don't mind. I would like an absolutely clear picture for counsel. We can do without the axe, of course.

LOTTE: You'll have to. The police removed it.

LETTICE: (*Seizing the property sword from the wall*) Never mind – I'll use this instead! It's a bit blunt but you can imagine it sharp . . . Lotte? Please! . . . It'll help me very much . . . *Please!* . . .

(*Glaring,* LOTTE *shrugs and rises under protest.*)

LOTTE: Go on, then.

LETTICE: She came forward on to the balcony where all was made ready – the whole scene draped in black. First she 'with her keener eye the axe's edge did try': that's Andrew Marvell – a true poet. Then she knelt down and looked up at me playing her hapless executioner – kneel, Lotte, please.

(LOTTE *kneels, tight-lipped.*)

Now speak your line. *Lotte!*

LOTTE: (*Swiftly*) Do not strike until I extend my hand so.

LETTICE: (*West Country accent*) Nay, I will not, an't please your Majesty.

LOTTE: (*As before*) Good fellow. I thank you.

(*She lies prone.*)

LETTICE: And then suddenly – suddenly I realized there was something wrong! . . . Do you know the most extraordinary fact about King Charles's execution? The headsman was so frightened of being identified by the mob – the man who actually struck the head off his monarch's shoulders – both he and his assistant appeared in total disguise. Not just in a mask – *a false beard and false hair.* Truly. (*To* LOTTE) I'm right, aren't I?

LOTTE: (*Prone*) For once.

LETTICE: Indeed some people said it was actually *Oliver Cromwell himself* disguised like that. I myself hardly dare believe it – *but what a story if it were true!* . . . Well anyway, I had totally forgotten to put them on. Can you believe such stupidity? – and it's the best thing about my whole part, the disguise. So I simply halted proceedings. Keeping dead in character, I said: (*West Country accent: confidential*) 'Excuse me, your Majesty. I foind I am without my foinal trappings. Pray give me leave to go and fetch 'em.' She nodded curtly, brilliantly taking up the cue – She nodded curtly, Lotte – (LOTTE *nods curtly*.) – and I scooted off into the bedroom to put them on. Like this.

(*She retreats backwards to the bedroom, bowing to her King all the way. She opens the bedroom door.* LOTTE *sits up in alarm*.)

LOTTE: *No! No!* Stop it now!

LETTICE: I can't! This is the best bit!

LOTTE: (*Panic in her voice*) Is she still there? Is she still in there?

LETTICE: Of course not! How could she be? . . . (*Irate*) Who did you think was going to look after her while I was in custody – *You?* . . . She was given away, the poor thing.

BARDOLPH: What are you talking about? I'm afraid I've lost you . . . You were getting your disguise.

LETTICE: I still am. And you are going to help me.

BARDOLPH: I?!

LETTICE: You're going to be the drums. I had to do them myself last time and it didn't work at all. Now you can fill in while I dress.

BARDOLPH: I couldn't.

LETTICE: Of course you can. It's just a sound.

BARDOLPH: No, I really couldn't!

LETTICE: You *must*, or we'll lose all the tension! Imagine them – beating all down Whitehall, hundreds of drums, without remorse of voice! . . . Pam-tititi-pam! . . . Pam-tititi-pam! . . . (*Pleading*) Try it, Mr Bardolph. It can really be thrilling if you do it properly . . . Won't you – *please?* . . . (*Showing him, with solemn hand gestures*) *Pam-tititi-pam! . . . Pam-tititi-pam!*

BARDOLPH: (*Imitating reluctantly and off the beat*) Pam-tititi-pam . . . Pam-tititi-pam . . .

(LETTICE *shakes her head.*)

LETTICE: More menace. It has to have more menace . . . Remember these were the most dreadful drums in England. They were announcing the end of everything.

BARDOLPH: What do you mean?

LETTICE: All the colour! The age of colour! The painted churches! The painted statues! The painted language! They're all about to go for ever – at one stroke of an axe! In their place will come grey! The great English grey! The grey of Cromwell's clothes! The grey of Prose and Puritanism, falling on us like a blight for ever! (*Pause.*) Play your role, Mr Bardolph. It is a great one! The honest yeoman wearing the helmet and breastplate against his will – beating out on his drum the end of old England! . . . Let them hear it now! Fill the snowy streets of London with it! (*Louder*) *Pam-tititi-pam! . . . Pam-tititi-pam!* . . . Come on now, Mr Bardolph – steady and terrible! *Pam-tititi-pam! . . . Pam-tititi-pam!*

(*Seduced,* BARDOLPH *joins in.*)

BARDOLPH: Pam-tititi-pam! Pam-tititi-pam!

LETTICE: That's *it*! *Excellent!* . . . Steady and terrible that's the secret . . . steady and terrible!

BARDOLPH: (*Growing more and more committed*) Pam-tititi-pam! . . . Pam-tititi-pam!

LETTICE: Bravo!

(*Suddenly he begins to march around the room to his own beat.* LOTTE, *on her knees, stares at him dumbfounded.*)

(*Clapping; delighted*) Bravo, Mr Bardolph! Well done . . . Keep it up! . . . *Let all England hear you!*

(*She watches for a second – then slips into the bedroom as the lawyer, transported, moves uninhibitedly around the room at a slow and menacing march, banging his invisible drum and calling out his* pam-tititi-pams *with increasing excitement.* LOTTE *watches in amazement. Suddenly from the bedroom we hear* LETTICE*'s voice join his in wild soprano doubling. Their noise rises in a crescendo.*)

BARDOLPH/LETTICE: Pam-tititi-pam! . . . Pam-tititi-pam! . . . Pam-tititi-pam! . . . Pam-tititi-pam!!!

(*Abruptly the duet breaks off.* LETTICE *has reappeared. She stands before the astonished lawyer in her disguise, holding the sword at attention with both hands. She wears her black Mary Queen of Scots cloak, only back to front; over her eyes is a black executioner's mask: over her chin is a false ginger beard: over her head, completing an appearance of the utmost grotesqueness, is* LOTTE*'s discarded and of course ill-fitting wig.* BARDOLPH *stares at her, open-mouthed.* LOTTE *turns away, refusing to look. A pause.*)

LETTICE: Never forget the most brilliant period in English history was brought to an end by a man looking like this. (*She advances into the room.*) The rest is quick to tell. I raised the axe – (*Demonstrating with the sword*) – and *she* came in! . . . I'd forgotten, you see, to close this door.

BARDOLPH: Who? Who came in?

LETTICE: Felina, Queen of Sorrows.

BARDOLPH: *Who?*

LETTICE: My cat. Lotte is terrified of cats. And of course Felina, the wicked thing, knew it. She bounded in – saw Lotte there on the floor – and simply jumped with all claws – right on top of her. Like this – MIAOW!

(LETTICE *jumps on* LOTTE *with claws extended.* LOTTE *jumps up in shock.*)

LOTTE: *Get off!* . . .

(LETTICE *drops the sword.*)

LETTICE: Poor Lotte jerked right up in the air! I was so startled I dropped the axe right on her. Just like that! It was dreadful! . . . Oh, it was so dreadful! . . . There was blood everywhere! She was moaning and crying, and suddenly there was this banging on the door . . . I couldn't get up and answer it – she was in such a state! I was trying to quiet her – and then the door just burst open and fell in. Exactly as you see it now.

BARDOLPH: And there was a policeman.

LETTICE: Yes . . . The rest you know.

(*A long pause.* MR BARDOLPH *wipes his brow with his handkerchief.*)

BARDOLPH: Well . . . (*To* LOTTE) There's only one thing you can do, I'm afraid. You'll have to turn hostile.

LOTTE: I beg your pardon?

BARDOLPH: It's a phrase. Since you are the prosecution witness you'll have to go into the box. Miss Douffet's counsel will cross-examine you. On your oath you must tell him precisely what I've just heard. That's what's called 'turning hostile witness'. The prosecution will of course ask the judge to take appropriate action.

LOTTE: Which is what?

BARDOLPH: To release Miss Douffet. There's obviously no case to answer.

(*He puts away the tape-recorder in his briefcase.*)

LOTTE: And that's all?

BARDOLPH: He may permit himself a few pleasantries at your expense . . . An Englishwoman's home is her scaffold – and so forth. You know judges . . . If it's Justice Gasgoine, which I think it may well be, things could be a little rougher.

LOTTE: What do you mean?

BARDOLPH: He'll almost certainly give you a lecture about wasting the time of the court. (*Very dry voice*) 'I find it extraordinary that two ladies of mature years have nothing better to do than behave like a couple of feeble-witted schoolgirls.' That kind of thing.

LOTTE: Yes. I see. Thank you.

(*She looks grimly at* LETTICE *who flinches.*)

Are you done here now?

BARDOLPH: I think so. Telephone me in the morning, Miss Douffet, if you would. I cannot of course call you.

LETTICE: (*Looking at* LOTTE; *subdued*) Yes.

BARDOLPH: Well, goodbye. I'll have all this written up and sent round to your counsel. With a note, of course.

LETTICE: Yes.

(*He goes to the stairs.*)

BARDOLPH: At least you won't have to go to prison. That's comforting, isn't it? A little embarrassment and it's all over.

LETTICE: All over, yes . . .

LOTTE: (*Cold*) Goodbye, Mr Bardolph.

BARDOLPH: Goodbye . . . Goodbye, Miss Douffet . . .

(*He extends his hand. She takes it. He tries to convey his sense of pleasure in having encountered her.*)

I – I – I really . . . (*But cannot.*) Goodbye.

(*He goes, hastily, taking his briefcase. We see his legs disappear upstairs. A pause. The two ladies stand, not looking at each other. The front door slams.* MR BARDOLPH*'s legs come down the front steps above and walk past the house out of sight.*)

LETTICE: You're very angry, aren't you?

LOTTE: (*Very cold*) Why should I be angry? A woman whose life has just been ruined.

LETTICE: (*Timid*) That's not absolutely true.

LOTTE: Not? How else would you put it?

LETTICE: All he said was 'a little embarrassment'. That's not ruin.

LOTTE: I was promoted last week. I am now Head of the Department.

LETTICE: (*Pleased*) Oh!

LOTTE: When this comes out I shall be its laughing stock. In fact, the laughing stock of London, when they read their papers . . . We both will be: but in your case it scarcely matters, does it?

LETTICE: (*Shocked*) Lotte!

LOTTE: I am a respected woman in a responsible and enviable job. After the trial I'll never be able to enter my office again . . . I will resign first thing in the morning.

LETTICE: No!

LOTTE: What else would you advise? Stay on and ignore the giggles? Pretend not to hear the whispers? You've done for me, Lettice. It's only just: I recognize that. Tit for tat. Perfect justice.

LETTICE: What are you talking about?

LOTTE: I dismiss you. You dismiss me. Revenge is sweet.

LETTICE: That's not fair!

LOTTE: It's absolutely right!

LETTICE: That's not fair at all!

LOTTE: *Fair?!* I join you, my dear, in the ranks of the Unemployed! Where I believe fairness is not the salient characteristic! Or I could sell tea towels in one of our remoter gift shops.

(*She gives* LETTICE *a ghastly smile. A bitter pause.*)

Actually I deserve it. I deserve it all. I let you do it.

LETTICE: Do what?

LOTTE: Lure me.

LETTICE: Lure?

LOTTE: Into your world. An actress's world. (*Harshly*) No – *not even an actress!* . . . Here.

(*She takes the keys of the flat out of her bag and drops them on the Falstaff chair.*)

LETTICE: You must know I am guiltless. Unwittingly I have brought embarrassment on you. That seems to be my allotted role – but it is not my purpose. Revile me if you wish. Spurn me, I don't blame you. Only know – I – I would truly sooner cut this hand off than injure one hair – one single hair in that corolla of grey!

LOTTE: Oh, stop it! STOP IT! Listen to yourself! 'Guiltless' . . . 'Spurn' . . . 'Revile' . . . 'Corolla'! . . . *Who are you being now?*

(*A pause.* LETTICE *looks at her, bewildered.*)

LETTICE: (*Simply*) Myself . . . Myself.

(*A pause.*)

LOTTE: (*Factual*) Let's not go on. It's entirely my fault. If one embraces the ridiculous, one ends up becoming ridiculous.

LETTICE: (*Stricken*) Don't!

LOTTE: That's all there is to it. Goodbye.

(*She goes up the stairs.*)

LETTICE: No!

(*She runs after her and calls up desperately from the bottom stair.*)

No. *You wanted it*. You said so often. 'That awful desk – the *Non-doer's Desk*. If only I could leave it and never see it again!'

(LOTTE *pauses.*)

You said that over and over!

LOTTE: (*Hard*) So you decided to give me a push, is that it? *Thank you!*

(*She goes on upstairs and out of the flat.*)

LETTICE: *Lotte!*

(*The front door slams.* LETTICE *looks about in panic, then dashes to the intercom telephone and picks it up. We see* LOTTE*'s legs starting to walk across the window, but* LETTICE*'s voice makes them halt.*)

(*Into the phone*) No! No, that's stupid – just *going*! We can think of *something* for you! There's always something! Even for *me* – there's *something*!

(*A pause.*)

(*In a voice of sudden defeat*) No. Actually, no . . . *Not* for me . . . (*Pause.*) You're wrong when you say there's nothing Ghosty about me. That's what *I am*. A Ghost. Every day more. Every day there's something new I don't understand . . . It's like a mesh keeping me out – all the new things, *your* things. Computers. Screens. Bleeps and buttons. Processors. Every day more . . . Bank cards – phone cards – software! JVC. PLC. ABC. DEF. (*More and more anguished*) The whole place – the whole world I understood isn't there . . . You talk about Europe gone – that's just buildings! *Everything*'s gone for me. I can't work any of it. *I*'m the foreigner – not Mr Pachmani. It's all like that writing on my walls – just squiggles and dots. (*Flatly*) You're right. That's the precise word for me – ridiculous. Ridiculous and useless. (*Pause.*) Useless stories. Useless glories. Ridiculous and useless. (*Pause.*) I'm sorry. I haven't got anything else.

(*Abruptly she hangs up the receiver, and stands crying helplessly. Equally abruptly* LOTTE *returns to the front door and presses the buzzer aggressively.* LETTICE *ignores it – but* LOTTE *insists. Finally* LETTICE *picks up the phone.*)

What?

LOTTE: (*Over: sharply*) Let me in!

LETTICE: No.

LOTTE: (*Over*) Do you hear me? Let me in at once. *Open it, Lettice.* (*Shouting*) *Press the damn thing!*

(LETTICE *presses the button. The front door opens above and slams.* LOTTE *storms down the stairs in outrage. She turns on the light at the bottom, making* LETTICE *shrink in its glare.*)

How dare you? That's disgusting. Snivelling, feeble, whining rubbish! That's not you! *I won't have it. I won't stand for it – do you hear?*

(LETTICE *turns away, hiding her head from the onslaught.*)

All right, I hated the job. You're right: I admit it. I'm glad to be done with it – all right! That doesn't mean I'm going to spend the rest of my life hiding in the Past . . . Are you listening?

LETTICE: (*Not looking at her*) I don't hide.

LOTTE: Of course you do. You're like those women in my office. (*'Refined' voice*) '*Oh, dear!* Oh *dear, dear, dear* – this horrid, nasty *Present*!' (*Hard*) The Past was just as nasty as we are. Just as stupid. Just as greedy and brutal.

LETTICE: No!

LOTTE: *Worse*. For most people it was far worse.

LETTICE: (*Hotly*) At least it was *beautiful*! You said that yourself. 'It gets uglier every minute,' you said.

LOTTE: So it does.

LETTICE: So why *shouldn't* I hide? It's hideous here. Everywhere . . . Hideous and hateful.

LOTTE: Then do something about it! *Fight it. Attack it*. Show some *spunk*, for God's sake! Don't just stay cringing in a basement, playing stupid games.

LETTICE: (*Desperate*) Well, what can I *do*? What can *you* do? Or anyone?

LOTTE: We are two able, intelligent women. I am an experienced organizer of tours. You are the most original tour guide. That must suggest something.

LETTICE: What?

LOTTE: We're a combination.

LETTICE: What do you *mean*?

LOTTE: (*Growing excited*) I have it! . . . Look – do you remember the E.N.D.? The 'Eyesore Negation Detachment'? (LETTICE *nods*.) Well, what if we revived it? In another form! Not bombs – *tours*! Why don't we start our own firm – E.N.D. Tours – dedicated to showing people *the fifty ugliest new buildings in London*? How about that? I can provide the architectural information – you can speak it in your own inimitable way! You lit up the Past with a blazing torch, people said. Well, now light up the Present! Reveal the ugliness for what it is!

LETTICE: Oh, Lotte!

LOTTE: I could advertise everywhere! Send leaflets into every travel agency in Britain, even America – why not? No one will have seen anything like it! (*Theatrically*) 'E.N.D. Tours Presents Lettice Douffet's Dramatic Guide to Disgusting Buildings! Hear her Devastating Denunciations of Modern

Design! Before your very eyes she will show you how Beauty has been Murdered – and by whom! Exactly which Architects, Builders, Engineers and City Planners!'

LETTICE: Oh, that's marvellous!

LOTTE: It could be!

LETTICE: (*Transported*) It's tremendous! It's the single most *theatrical* idea I ever heard! (*Ardently*) *My mother would have been so proud of you!* (*Pause.*) Let's imagine it – how it could go . . . We're in some vast, horrible office building, surrounded by a huge group of tourists – hanging on my every word . . . Let's see!

(*Gleefully she addresses her imaginary audience.*)

You are standing now in the Main Hall of . . . Computex House.

LOTTE: Splendid! Computex House!

LETTICE: Constructed in 1980 out of British concrete. Observe the cracks, splits and damp stains typical of the period.

(LOTTE *laughs.*)

The obvious intention of this building is to resemble as much as possible a top-security prison. Note the thousand metal-framed windows – not one of which can be opened.

LOTTE: And made out of black solar glass – that's the name.

LETTICE: Substituting for the ghastly glow of sunshine the glorious glare of fluorescence!

LOTTE: The architect responsible was awarded a knighthood last year for his brilliant contribution to the environment.

(LETTICE *goes to the stairs, and takes her position as in Act One.*)

LETTICE: This object is the Central Staircase, consisting of five hundred steps in artificial stone.

LOTTE: Granolithic compound, please.

LETTICE: Thank you. Notice how its steel banisters adroitly suggest the idea of Incarceration.

(LOTTE *laughs.* LETTICE *includes the audience out front more directly.*)

You may like to know that these grim stairs were recently the scene of the most dramatic protest yet to be made by ordinary people against British brutalist architecture. Last Christmas Eve – a brilliant snowy night, although nobody inside could see it because of the solar glass – six Filing Clerks, unable to bear the prospect of working in this place another day, walked up all five hundred grey and granolithic steps – joined hands on the topmost landing up there (*She points upwards*) and together hurled themselves into the stairwell below, singing the Hallelujah Chorus. They landed precisely where I stand now! . . . For this reason it is now known as the Staircase of Secretarial Solace.

LOTTE: (*Laughing*) You are incorrigible! You really are!

LETTICE: And you're *dazzling*, Lotte! It's a dazzling idea! We'll make a fortune!

LOTTE: Wait! I have a perfect thought for the end. When you finish – just before you dismiss them – we give them all a present. Something they won't be expecting.

LETTICE: What?

(*Chuckling,* LOTTE *runs off into the kitchen and returns instantly with a tray bearing the two jewelled goblets and a bottle of Quaff.*)

LOTTE: (*Holding it aloft*) Ladies and gentlemen, E.N.D. Tours take pride in offering you a complimentary beverage after the aesthetic horrors you have endured!

LETTICE: Oh, wonderful!

(LOTTE *sets down the tray and pours.*)

LOTTE: Please drink deep. This cordial is not meant to trickle down the throat but to cascade.

LETTICE: Bravo! That's perfect.

LOTTE: And then I'll say, 'It is entirely the inspiration of my colleague, Miss Lettice Douffet, a lady of countless inspirations. (*To the audience out front*) It offers in miniature what she herself offers in bounteous measure. Enlargement for shrunken souls. Enlivenment for dying spirits. Enlightenment for dim, prosaic eyes. (*Pause.*) In short – lovage.'

(*Music sounds, antique and tender.* LOTTE *crosses the stage with the two goblets and solemnly hands one to* LETTICE, *standing at the bottom of the stairs.*)

LETTICE: (*Also looking out front*) This concludes our tour for today. On behalf of Miss Schoen and myself – a *brimming* goodbye to you!

(*The two ladies toast the audience. The curtain falls.*)

YONADAB

Inspired by the novel The Rape of Tamar
by Dan Jacobson

For
Frank,
with love

CHARACTERS

YONADAB, nephew of King David
DAVID, King of Judah and Israel
AMNON, David's eldest son
ABSALOM, David's favourite son
TAMAR, David's only daughter
MICAH, waiting-woman to Tamar

SIX HELPERS

★

The action of the play takes place in the City of Jerusalem. The time: 1000 BC.

The set consists of a stage within a stage. These are referred to throughout the text as the inner stage or the outer stage.

Seated motionless around the outer stage before the play begins are the HELPERS. *These are six figures in white robes: their individual features are obliterated by white stocking masks. During the performance these* HELPERS *take all the parts in the play other than those named in the List of Characters: David's other sons; Absalom's bodyguards; priests, porters, servants, and the people of Jerusalem, both men and women. They are all-purpose assistants: they make sounds, but they never speak dialogue. Their gestures are informed with a clearly read, graphic authority.*

It is expected that sound in general will be produced with great variety and virtuosity through speakers in the auditorium, greatly supplementing what is provided by the Helpers on stage.

Yonadab was first performed at the Olivier Theatre on 4 December 1985, with the following cast:

YONADAB, nephew of King David	Alan Bates
SHIMEAH, his father	Richard Warner
DAVID, King of Judah and Israel	Patrick Stewart
AMNON, David's eldest son	Leigh Lawson
ABSALOM, David's favourite son	Anthony Head
TAMAR, David's only daughter	Wendy Morgan
MICAH, waiting-woman to Tamar	Janet Whiteside
PRIEST	Brian Spink
AMNON'S BONDSMEN	Robert Arnold
	Peter Dineen
ABSALOM'S GUARDS	Robert Arnold
	Ben Bazell
	Peter Dineen
	John Priestley
KING DAVID'S OTHER SONS	Stephen Coke
	Mark Dowse
	Gordon Kane
	Robert Ralph
	Peter Tate
KING DAVID'S SERVANTS	Nola Haynes
	Tacy Kneale

Other parts played by members of the company

DIRECTOR	Peter Hall
DESIGN AND LIGHTING	John Bury
MUSIC	Dominic Muldowney
MOVEMENT	Elizabeth Keen

ACT ONE

SCENE ONE

A remote music. YONADAB *appears: a man in early middle age wearing the robes of his tribe. Darkness behind him.*

YONADAB: (*To audience*) *Voolamnown rayah vooshomov Yonadab.* 'And Amnon had a friend whose name was Yonadab.' *V'Yonadab eese hochom m'owd.* 'And Yonadab was a very subtle man.' Meaning devious – the usual adjective used in my tribe for anyone of intelligence. Not often employed, as a result. I am quoting the Authorized Version of your Bible, Second Book of Samuel, Chapter Thirteen. It gives me two mentions – one as cunning, one as kind – creating between them a kind of invisibility. Highly appropriate for me, as a matter of fact.
(*Pause.*)
This is a singularly unpleasant story. The Rabbis of the Middle Ages omitted it entirely, when they read out the scriptures, to spare the ears of their congregations – and they didn't know the half of it. I alone know it all – and, let me assure you, I don't intend to spare yours. One does not live in limbo for eternity, my dears, in order to spare people.
(*Pause.*)
This is a tale of total deceit. Every person in it both deceiver and deceived. And I mean every single one. It is the true and secret story of the ruin of the House of David by me – his despised nephew. Yonadab the Despised, son of Shimeah the Ignored – passed over by the tetchy old Prophet Samuel when he anointed Dad's younger brother while still a stripling to be King over the tribes of Judah and Israel.

(*Lights up on* DAVID, *sitting on his throne on the inner stage.*)
David ben Jesse, my tremendous uncle! – strongest figure in the world three thousand years ago. Gracious, audacious, mendacious, salacious David – sent by Yaveh, the One God, to rule his Chosen Race – famous People of the tablets! You, to whom tablets mean something altogether more comforting and easily absorbed, cannot imagine their effect on a tribe fully as ferocious as its neighbours.
(*Four* HELPERS *move slowly to kneel before* DAVID *as bound prisoners. Two others stand behind them as priests.*)
Banish from your minds all images of cowed men cringing in ghettos, or kind men creating cultural centres. We were not cringers then – or kind. We were smiters! We smote the whole world in the name of our God of Commandment. Ammonites, Canaanites, Jebusites, Amalekites, Hivites, Hittites, Perizites, Moabites – all the Ites in fact whom you now cannot tell apart because we smote them so completely. I feel no particular regret for these Ites: they were largely beastly – and even more beastly were the mighty kingdoms shadowing us, Babylon and Assyria. Just don't make the mistake of imagining David as a gentle ex-shepherd always lying down in green pastures. His pasture was a stony city on a stony hill. And ten commandments of stone were permanently on his tongue.

DAVID: (*Sternly*) These men are foes of the One God: wherefore they die. Let them be taken to the Place of Stones, and there let stones be cast upon them till they be broken into death. Selah.
(*The two* PRIESTS *raise their hands.*)
I say to you, blessed is he who serves the Lord. Cursed is he who sets his hand against Him or His anointed. There shall not be left one such in my seeing to piss against the wall. So also and more do God to me if I neglect one letter of His commandments unto you. Selah.
(*He claps his hands. A fierce drumming is heard. The two* PRIESTS *stone in mime the four kneeling* MEN *who fall forward, dead. In the theatre the audience hears the sounds of the tribe crying out approval, against the shrill sound of rams' horns being blown. Light changes.*

The stoners go off. The dead remain lying on the outer stage.)

YONADAB: (*To audience*) It was like that every day in Jerusalem. The air stank of blood. Human blood in the gutters: animal blood from the altars. And beyond in the desert, for miles, the blood of our chopped enemies soaking the sand. I sicked up daily from the stench. The thing was, you see, alone in all the tribe I was delicate. That is actually my main defence for all the horror that follows. I was delicate: God clearly was not. How could He possibly have made me in His image? I saw no resemblance. Here was Yonadab the Sensitive – there was Yaveh the Savage, with no female consort to soften Him and not one trace of humour to keep Him in temper. That is, if He was there at all. (*Lowering his voice*) To say to you what I did not even dare hint when alive, I was not totally convinced of this terrifying fact. The Bible-readers amongst you no doubt assume that everyone in ancient Israel was a ramping, stamping Believer. Not true. That's propaganda. For a start, there was me. Yonadab the Creep. That actually is what you become when you bow to One God because you're terrified of stones – but long in your heart for another one altogether, who has no use for stones. To put it bluntly, this religion was simply not good enough for me.

(*The four dead prisoners rise* –)

DAVID: Let my sons approach. Bring them food.

(– *and become* ADONIJAH, ITHREAM, SHEPATIAH *and* SHOBAB. *The other two* HELPERS *enter as servants with dishes of food*.)

YONADAB: (*To audience*) Let's join them for lunch, where the story really begins. And be glad you're not eating it. The food, being prepared under the strict supervision of priests without the slightest knowledge of gastronomy, was quite simply horrendous. Indigestion was a permanent condition one thousand years BC. (*He steps on to the inner stage*.) Incidentally, 'C' – being descended from David – is also one of *my* family connections.

DAVID: (*With a greeting gesture*) Adonijah. Ithream.

(*They bow to their father.* YONADAB *eagerly bows to them – and is ignored*.)

Shobab. Shepatiah.

(*The same thing happens. The* SONS *sit. The two* SERVANTS *hold up the bowls of food to be blessed by the king.*)

YONADAB: There were actually more sons – equally faceless. David's ghastly brood: ambitious, dark-souled bullies, scared of Daddy, licensed to sneer at me: and every one of them watching the old man for signs of failing.

(DAVID *rises. All prostrate themselves, including* YONADAB.)

DAVID: (*Extending his hand over the food*) Blessed art Thou, King of the Universe, who hast given us bread from the earth! (*With a slight menace*) And blessed be he who eats it in peace with his brothers. In whose heart is no secret thing. (*He stares at them hard.*) Eat and be satisfied.

(*The two* SERVANTS *place the bowls before the* BROTHERS *and retire on to the outer stage. The* BROTHERS *eat. So does* YONADAB, *dipping his hand into the communal bowl.*)

YONADAB: (*To audience*) Some years before, David had had a Hittite man killed in order to possess his wife, Bathsheba. It was said that as a punishment God killed the first son they had together – and then placed a sword for ever in the midst of his other children. You may judge for yourselves how true this was, tonight.

(*The light changes. The two* HELPERS *on the outer stage now assume hieratic poses suggestive of Egyptian god-figures: one male, one female. The* SONS *on the inner stage bow over their food. An exotic music sounds.*)

As long as I could remember I had yearned to escape from the world of perpetual anger which was Jerusalem. Every night I would slip home to my tiny bedroom in a backstreet, and dream. As a boy someone had told me the Legend of the Kingdom of Perpetual Peace which once had been in the distant past – ruled over jointly by a King and Queen, young and deep in love. Both beautiful – and both immortal.

(*The* FIGURES *embrace tenderly.*)

A place where flutes filled the air – not the squeal of rams' horns, or rams themselves dragged shitting to slaughter for a ravenous God. A place where walls showed pictures of undying pleasure – not simply letters of proscription, *Thou*

Shalt Not! A place not simply glared over by a ferocious Judge but smiled on by this radiant couple, filling their worshippers with the scent of their joy.

(*The two* FIGURES *go slowly offstage, arm in arm.*)

Some nights I could actually see his exquisite brown shoulders – her vivid turquoise eyes under the lids of my own . . . It was a totally imbecile fantasy, I admit. Far more to do with sex than celestial matters – and far far too soft a myth for the ruffians around me. All the same – it gave one a little comfort in this place of fear and duty.

SCENE TWO

Light changes.

AMNON *and* ABSALOM *come in from either side.* AMNON *is a man in his early thirties, stocky and powerful – 'thick' in several senses of the word – and at this moment is noticeably distracted. By contrast* ABSALOM *in his early twenties is a glorious beauty – handsome and well tended, with a spectacular mane of black hair, at present tied up. There is something innocent and engagingly stupid about* AMNON: *something ardently emotional and yet dangerous and immature about* ABSALOM, *who enters accompanied by two of his guards carrying staves of wood with which they bang on the ground to signify opinion.*

YONADAB: Here come the only two sons you need to bother with.

DAVID: Absalom! The Shiner!

ABSALOM: (*Fervently*) May your days fatten for ever, Beloved Father!

YONADAB: Absalom the Favourite. The only one permitted to have a private guard. Popular and shining as the sun – he is yet, like that star, finally impossible to see into. (*Bowing to him*) My lord Prince.

(ABSALOM *ignores him.*)

DAVID: Amnon!

AMNON: (*Nodding but not bowing*) May your days fatten, Father.

DAVID: What? I couldn't hear.

AMNON: (*Louder, sullen*) May your days fatten, beloved Father.

DAVID: I thank you.

YONADAB: Amnon the Firstborn – known as the Bull. My only friend and protector. The sort of powerful fool an intelligent creep really needs in a place like this.

(AMNON *summons* YONADAB *to him with a jerk of the head. He rises and goes to him.*)

Like all bulls he is deeply lecherous. But, unlike them, he is also pretentious. An odd combination. His one real desire is to be thought profound. Luckily for me he regards me as a scholar. Which by his booby standards I suppose I am. (*To* AMNON; *obsequiously*) My Prince.

AMNON: (*Testy; sotto voce*) Where have you been?

YONADAB: Family business; on our estate. I declare there is no more boring place on earth than Galilee.

AMNON: I required you.

YONADAB: I'm sorry.

AMNON: Come to me tonight.

YONADAB: If I can.

AMNON: No 'if'! Come. (*Sharply*) *Am I heard?*

YONADAB: (*Surprised*) You certainly are! (*To audience*) Something was clearly up. I'd never seen him so disordered.

DAVID: Amnon!

AMNON: Ha?

DAVID: Come here. What is it with you today? Are you sick? Look into my face. (*He takes it in his hand.*) Is it drink?

AMNON: No.

DAVID: 'No'? To whom do you speak?

AMNON: (*Sulkily*) Beloved Father.

DAVID: Whores, then?

AMNON: No, Beloved Father.

DAVID: I think *yes*! (*Amused*) You've been at it!

AMNON: I have not. I swear it!

DAVID: Don't swear to falsehood.

AMNON: I have been with no women, Father!

DAVID: For how long?

AMNON: (*Embarrassed and angry*) Long! A month – two months – I don't know.

(*The* PRINCES *make mocking noises at him.*)

(*Furiously; to them*) I say long! I do not need women every hour like you. I consider the mind! The *mind* – what you haven't got!

(*The* PRINCES *bang the floor, delighted.*)

DAVID: Tsss! You're a bull first – a mighty bull! Leave mind to Absalom! (*To* ABSALOM) Tell us your opinion, my Shiner. Does he speak truth?

ABSALOM: How should I know, Great Father? He is so hidden from us. We never see him, do we?

AMNON: What do you mean?

ABSALOM: When were you last at court?

AMNON: I'm not on display all day – that's true!

(*The* PRINCES *laugh.*)

DAVID: Tsss! Enough! It is your right to be dark and hidden, if you wish. Just as it is Absalom's to be open and shining. (*To* ABSALOM) How may I please you today, my Shining boy? Tell me the reward for open-ness!

ABSALOM: There is nothing I want, Beloved Father!

DAVID: That I can't believe. There isn't a boy amongst you who doesn't want something from the King.

ABSALOM: There is one thing, I confess.

DAVID: Ah-ha!

ABSALOM: For you to be my guest at Ba'al Hazoor. Next month will be the Feast of Tabernacles. You haven't been in the country for years. The people long to see you! Am I right, men?

(*His* GUARDS *bang their staves in confirmation.*)

If you come, I'll *fill* my fields with tabernacles! – a hundred! A thousand tents!

(*The staves bang. He salutes his father. Freeze.*)

YONADAB: (*To audience*) He issues this invitation to the country several times a year. And each time David has to find another reason for refusing. He is far too suspicious ever to leave his capital.

DAVID: My lovely boy, a King cannot do as he pleases. When he travels the people expect a show. They want to say, 'Look, what might attends our ruler!'

ABSALOM: You may bring as many as you wish, Great Father. My estate is large thanks only to your bounty!

DAVID: The Lord forbid I should require beggary from my children as proof of love!

ABSALOM: It would not be beggary, Father.

DAVID: Never! Never!

ABSALOM: But, Father, I implore you –

DAVID: (*Savagely*) *Not another word!* Come here – (*Recovering*) To my heart! Hear how it beats for you!

(*He opens his arms and enfolds his son.* PRINCES *and* GUARDS *make the noise of approval.*)

Such a beauty here! Who would believe such a beauty could come from the loins of an ugly thing like me?

ABSALOM: (*Embarrassed*) Father . . .

DAVID: I ask you all – when have you seen hair like this – yes, even on your ladies? No, no, no – permit your father! (*He handles the famous hair, but does not unloose it.*) Do you know, when he cut it off at this year's end, how much it weighed? He wouldn't tell you – he's too modest – but I sent spies to find out! Shall I tell you? Two hundred shekels! *Two hundred shekels – King's weight!* Who ever heard of hair like this on any head in Israel?

(*The staves bang; the* PRINCES *dutifully applaud.* AMNON *turns away.*)

Oh, don't frown there, Amnon! What is it? – jealous? Foolish fellow! (*He rises from his throne and goes to him.*) I love you as a father can only love his first-seen son! You are my bull! My big bull son! *Ha!* (*He imitates horns and charging motions.*) Choo-choo! . . . Ha! . . . Haaa!

(*He stamps the ground and pokes at* AMNON *with his horns.* AMNON *shakes him off angrily. The* PRINCES *hiss. Silence falls.*)

Oh. (*Dangerous*) Well. He's not to be amused today, our bull. Tch, tch, tch . . . So then – where's my girl? You boys have been praised enough. You're all spoilt. Where's Tamar? I'll see my Tamar. Where is she? Absalom!

ABSALOM: She's outside, waiting your call.

DAVID: (*Affecting doubt*) No! Do you swear this?

ABSALOM: Would I deceive you, Beloved King?

DAVID: Never! Let her come in! She will refresh us all! (*Calling*) Tamar! (*Coyly*) Tamar? Where are you? *Tamar!* We long for you! Help me, boys!

(*The* PRINCES *bang their hands on the floor, like an audience impatient for a show to begin. The* GUARDS *join in with their staves. Suddenly a chord of music. All freeze.*)

YONADAB: (*To audience*) And now, my dears, for the Sex Interest in this story. Its subject – its scandal – its total cause! Primped and perfumed for the purpose – released from the Palace Harem to wait on her besotted father – full sister to Absalom, half-sister to Amnon, the old man's only daughter: *Tamar.* Single most spoilt creature in the Kingdom.

(*Music.* TAMAR *enters and curtsies demurely to* DAVID. *She is young and deeply attractive.*)

Intolerable Princess. Hateful little girl, for whom I was too low to notice.

(DAVID *raises her veil.*)

DAVID: Perfection! I shall declare it! I'll have it inscribed on tablets of porphyry: 'The Lord blessed his issue with perfection!'

(*The* PRINCES *bang the floor.*)

Here, my joy. The sweetest morsel!

(*He offers a cake with his fingers.*)

TAMAR: Blessing first.

DAVID: What?

TAMAR: (*Priggishly*) You must always say the Blessing first: don't you know that?

DAVID: (*Amused*) Quite right. Good girl. (*He holds up the cake.*) 'Blessed art Thou, King of the Universe, who has given us bread from the earth.'

TAMAR: (*Piously*) Amen.

(*He pops the cake into her mouth.*)

DAVID: Now you must sing for us.

TAMAR: No.

DAVID: What?

TAMAR: I don't feel like it.

DAVID: But I've been looking forward to it all morning. We all have . . .

TAMAR: I'm sorry. I've no voice today.

DAVID: Of course you do. I see we have to coax you! Amnon, coax your sister. She'll do it for you.

(AMNON *seems not to hear.*)

Amnon!

AMNON: (*Low voice, not looking at her*) Sing, Tamar.

DAVID: What's that? You don't sound very sincere. You're begging a favour worth our entire Kingdom. People don't sing for the half-hearted, do they, my dove?

(ABSALOM *springs up.*)

ABSALOM: (*Ardently*) Sing, Tamar, I implore! Sing for *me*! I'll play for you!

DAVID: (*Sharply*) No. You lack the skill. I'll play myself. Give me the instrument!

(*Applause. The* KING *is given his lyre.* TAMAR *sits beside her father on the steps of the throne. The* KING *strikes the instrument softly: softly the girl echoes the note. Then music begins in earnest, and the girl starts to dance and sing – crooning and ululating as she flirts with her brothers. She pays particular attention to* ABSALOM, *for a while pointedly ignoring* AMNON, *but gradually she works her way over to where he sits brooding. One touch of her veil upon the Bull's face, and he almost faints. In his frenzy he strikes out and smashes his dish. The song stops abruptly.* DAVID *breaks off playing. All the* PRINCES *stare.* AMNON *turns away.*)

(*With suppressed rage*) I think I'm right. My Bull has taken too much wine. Wine is not for bulls. It makes them clumsy. Go on, Tamar. Finish the song.

TAMAR: (*Pettishly*) No. I don't feel like it now. He's spoilt it.

(*She stamps her foot, throws her veil at* AMNON *and runs off.* DAVID *glares at his eldest son, hisses in fury, and stalks off.* ABSALOM *follows with his guards. The other* HELPERS *rise and take off the throne. The lights change. A canopy falls from above, edged with a fringe of opaque white curtains, rolled up tightly. This denotes:*)

SCENE THREE

Amnon's house. Sunset.

AMNON *moves and sits brooding.*

YONADAB: (*To audience*) But of course it wasn't wine. That was obvious. Suddenly I knew exactly. You know too, don't you, my dears? You saw what I saw. Something hardly to be thought of. Could it possibly be true? I went to his house that night hardly able to contain myself.

(*Two* HELPERS *return as Amnon's bondsmen, bowing before* YONADAB *and conducting him to* AMNON. YONADAB *steps on to the inner stage. The* BONDSMEN *depart.*)

(*To him*) Amnon?

AMNON: (*Dully*) Mmm.

YONADAB: I've come.

AMNON: Here.

(YONADAB *approaches warily.*)

Kneel.

(YONADAB *kneels.* AMNON *reveals a knife in his hand.*)

Cut.

YONADAB: What?

AMNON: Here. Now. Cut me.

YONADAB: Amnon!

AMNON: (*Grabbing his hand and forcing the knife into it, and to his own fork*) *Do it!* Cut me. Here! Do it!

YONADAB: (*Wrestling with* AMNON) Stop it! Stop it – no! (*He throws the knife far off.*) Stop this, Amnon! Give me words – not this!

(*Pause.*)

AMNON: No one must speak it, ever. No one! *Ever!*

YONADAB: *I* might.

(*Pause.*)

AMNON: What?

YONADAB: Will you swear not to hurt me if I speak? On your head?

(AMNON *touches his head in the gesture of oath.*)

(*Carefully*) There is a law in Israel. Thou shalt not uncover the nakedness of thy sister. Nor yet thy half-sister . . . (*Pause.*) Well?

AMNON: (*Whispering*) Yes.

YONADAB: How long has this been?

AMNON: For ever.

YONADAB: More exactly.

AMNON: A month! In the palace. She was singing that same song – snapping her fingers to the music. That's all! Snap, snap: then suddenly she was here, *in my head*. All day – all night! . . . As soon as I close my eyes she starts up whispering: 'Amnon! Amnon! I'm here! I'm with you! Amnon! Amnon!' I went to a wizard in secret. I asked him, 'Is there a demon can be raised just by snapping fingers?' He said, 'Yes.' I ordered him to cast it out. He put a Sign on me. Look! (*He tears open his shirt. On his chest a Sign is painted in vivid colours.*) He said not to wipe it clear for one month. *But it's no good!* It gets worse each night! Worse and worse . . .

YONADAB: Hush, Amnon. Hush now! Rest a moment. Here – on the breast of a friend.

(*He clasps* AMNON *to him.* AMNON *freezes.*)

(*To audience*) So close he filled my nose: the Bull rancid in chains. There and then a demon sprang up in *me*! The one which lives in the guts of all despised men waiting to be summoned. A lust greater even than the one in him: to bring things down. To make it happen – ruin! Ruin to the great who despise me! To the House of David for whom I didn't exist! Ruin even to the *God* of David! – why not? Let Him defend Himself! Prove that He exists, *finally*! *Let Him stop me* if He is there – Yaveh the Prohibitor! (*Pause.*) I opened my mouth, and it all began.

(AMNON *stirs and groans.*)

(*To him*) This may not be a demon, Amnon.

AMNON: What do you mean?

(YONADAB *rises.* AMNON *stays on the floor.*)

YONADAB: Your father regards you as mere muscle, but I know better. I have long thought of you as someone exceptional – you know that. Just how exceptional may now be the question.

AMNON: What are you saying?

YONADAB: It's hard. I fear to speak of it . . . But it just could be possible.

AMNON: What? Please! – *What?* (*Pause.*) *Please!*

YONADAB: I've told you often of a legend from long ago. The lost Kingdom of Perpetual Peace. Do you remember?

AMNON: Ruled over by a young King and Queen.

YONADAB: Deep in love.

AMNON: And both immortal.

YONADAB: Yes.

AMNON: What of it?

YONADAB: That King and Queen were brother and sister.
(*Pause.* AMNON *looks at him wide-eyed.*)
And in honour of that legend such union is still allowed in Egypt today.

AMNON: No!

YONADAB: It's true. Only to kings. And, of course, the sons of kings. No one else. But for them it is actually ordained.

AMNON: Ordained?

YONADAB: Expected. It's what actually makes them gods.

AMNON: What do you mean? What are you talking about?

YONADAB: The royal men of Egypt are all Gods. Don't you know that?

AMNON: Gods?

YONADAB: Certainly.

AMNON: Gods? (*Sniggering*) You're making this up!

YONADAB: Really, the Priests keep you in remarkable ignorance, Amnon.

AMNON: Gods? *Gods?*

YONADAB: Look: Yaveh shares His divinity with no one, not even a wife. But by the Nile it is all different! There, if you are a true prince, you are immortal. Immortality is your birthright. It is *inside* you, waiting to be born.
(AMNON *stops laughing.*)

AMNON: Born? How born?

YONADAB: In congress. With your sister.

AMNON: Congress? What's that – congress?

YONADAB: In bed.

AMNON: (*Shocked*) Tssss!

YONADAB: A holy bed, of course.

AMNON: Tsss! Tssssss! Abomination! That's abomination!

YONADAB: Unquestionably. I shouldn't have spoken.

AMNON: No, you shouldn't! (*Pause.*) Go on.

YONADAB: Forgive me, but it's too dangerous. We should leave it here.

AMNON: (*Springing up*) *Go on!* You can't leave it there!

YONADAB: I'm afraid. Truly . . .

AMNON: Look, you're a scholar. What would be blasphemy in ordinary people is – is learning in you. It's allowed. I allow it! In fact, I – *ordain* it! (*He laughs.*) It's your *duty* to speak! (*A pause.*)

YONADAB: (*Mysteriously*) Have you ever heard of a Choosing?

AMNON: Choosing?

YONADAB: In ancient legends a sister chooses one out of many brothers. Exactly as Samuel the Prophet chose your father. She comes to him in a vision and selects him to share eternal life with her.

AMNON: A vision! In the head?

YONADAB: Exactly. I have actually read certain old parchments – absolutely forbidden, of course. The process is amazing. An image of his sister is sent into the Prince's head by the Gods. She doesn't even know it herself. She then torments him.

AMNON: How?

YONADAB: With wooing. Whispering. Ogling. Tempting gestures . . .

AMNON: (*Avidly*) Go on!

YONADAB: He suffers horribly.

AMNON: Yes.

YONADAB: He writhes – he faints – he almost dies of it, apparently.

AMNON: Yes!

YONADAB: But in the end, if he is worthy, he wins through! They couple together with a pleasure unimaginable to the rest of mankind – and achieve Immortality! When they die, they both pass into another world, where they love each other for eternity.

(*Pause.* AMNON *looks at him suspiciously but deeply impressed.*)

AMNON: You don't believe this. You can't believe this yourself! . . . It's ridiculous, isn't it? It's just pure superstition, isn't it?

YONADAB: (*Coolly*) I am a scholar, Amnon, as you say. I merely tell you what has been believed by Egyptians. At the same time I must tell you – between you and me – they have the most profound society yet known. Far more so, my dear, than ours.

AMNON: Then what are you saying? What are you telling me?

YONADAB: Nothing. Actually, I think your wizard is right. This is almost certainly a demon that's plaguing you. But if by some astounding chance it is not – then the most miraculous thing is happening to you.

AMNON: A Choosing?

YONADAB: Yes. Incredible as that may seem.

AMNON: But . . . how do you tell which?

YONADAB: Only you can do that. (*Pause. Seriously*) Could you stay here in this room alone for seven days?

AMNON: Seven days!

YONADAB: That's how it's done. If you are truly royal, the old Gods will be inside you, waiting. You have to invoke them. Ask them directly: 'Is this a demon or is it Destiny?' They will reply through the girl's mouth. When the vision appears you will have to question her closely – allow no evasion. The act you dream of must be holy or let it never be done.

AMNON: (*Deeply impressed*) I never realized there were such depths in you!

YONADAB: If it is Demon, you must defy it. If Destiny – I promise I will help you fulfil it.

AMNON: How? The girl's locked up tight in the Palace!

YONADAB: Then I'll get her out of it. I promise you that. Even the plans of Gods have to be helped by men, you know.

AMNON: (*Fervently*) You're amazing! You're absolutely amazing, Yonadab! And how deep you are. To have kept all this hidden!

YONADAB: Remember this: you'll be acting for me, as well. We common men lie in our beds and finger ourselves. Princes make our dreams happen – or what is their use?

AMNON: (*Even more impressed*) Ah!

YONADAB: Seven days – alone. Do you think you can stand it?

AMNON: I am David's eldest son. I can stand anything.

YONADAB: Good man! (*They embrace. Then* AMNON *freezes. To audience:*) And off I went, straight to the country, away out of his reach. A week totally on his own would put the poor fool beyond any kind of reason!

SCENE FOUR

Light change. AMNON *kneels and puts over his head his amulet, kissing it elaborately. Four* HELPERS *come in bearing between them a litter on poles.* YONADAB *climbs into it and they lift it up, marching in place as porters on the outer stage.*

AMNON: Protect Thou me against all Devils, Spirits in the air, and flesh! Amen and Amen. Selah and Amen!

YONADAB: (*To audience*) As I journeyed down to our bleak estate I felt drunk. Ruin! Ruin! Ruin! Could I do it? Could I actually bring down the Lord's Anointed and his insufferable family? Or would He stop me – the Great Punisher above? What a test! What a marvellous, outrageous challenge! Let's see Who's really there!

AMNON: Tamar! Tamar! Come!

YONADAB: (*To audience*) All that week I sat with my visions, and he with his.

AMNON: Appear to me now – and stay!

YONADAB: (*To audience*) Mine were more disgusting, I admit. Tamar the immemorial daddy's girl, wriggling on her back.

AMNON: (*Putting on a serious voice*) Where art Thou? Speak within me!

YONADAB: (*To audience*) Not being hurt, you understand. No violence. Just dirt and dishonour. That lofty little Princess reduced for ever to the level I lived on every day.

AMNON: Plainer! Make me hear it!
(*He bows himself from the waist.*)

YONADAB: (*To audience*) Tamar the Insolent – join Yonadab the Insulted! Let her brothers sneer at *her* for a change!

AMNON: (*Bowing himself to and fro with increasing vigour*) Yes . . . Yes . . . O yes! Thy mouth! Thy mouth – O yes! And *yes*!

YONADAB: (*To audience*) The only problem was how to work it. Up to this point she had never once been out of the palace. Of course, the simplest plans are best, as you all know. And I flattered myself that mine – as I thought it up – was almost perfect in its simplicity.

AMNON: (*Swaying desperately*) More . . . More! More! I am Thy servant! Thy slave. Speak more!

(*The litter is lowered.* YONADAB *steps out of it, and it is borne off.*)

YONADAB: (*To audience*) He was right first time, of course. Lust like his *is* a demon. Its teeth beyond dislodging in the heart of the belly: its tongue soft as a girl's in the heart of the ear. It will make a man believe anything – especially a man like this. *Anything*, my dears. *Anything at all* – so long as it can be satisfied.

AMNON: (*Crying out*) Ah! Yes!! Yes!! I *know*!

(*He whirls on* YONADAB *as he re-enters the inner stage.*)

SCENE FIVE

Lights up.

AMNON: I know it all, Yonadab!

YONADAB: Yes?

AMNON: (*Wildly excited*) It's *true* – everything you said! You have no idea what I've endured! I thought I would die. Actually be broken in pieces. The Gods gave me strength – yes, you're right – *Gods!* There are many – hundreds – all around me! They spoke to me all the time – but through *her*! I could never have believed it possible! She appeared to me in a vision, clear as you! She used words she never uses, like 'Hearken'! 'Hearken, Amnon,' she said. 'I am thy sister come to tell thee tidings! There is a union forbidden to all but the most privileged. It alone can explain Desire! The feeling which forces Man over and over to do the same act, but never tells him what it's *for*! This will tell you! You are Chosen to know what only Gods know: (*impressive gesture*) the Meaning of Lusting!' . . . What do you think of that?

YONADAB: Incredible.

AMNON: Then she became specific. 'You will inherit,' she said. 'When our father dies – which will be soon now. Then we will reign together as husband and wife – shining on the land like the sun! It will be *Amnon* the Shiner, then – not Absalom! And the priests will be powerless to prevent it! . . . And when we die we will simply pass into another world together – and live for ever!'

YONADAB: She said all this?

AMNON: Yonadab – I heard it! Clear as you!

YONADAB: I believe you! Absolutely! I'm just – beyond words.

(AMNON *freezes.*)

(*To audience*) And so I *was* – absolutely! Who would believe this? A trickle of half-digested mysticism started by me had become in him a river of drivel! One night of sex was going to make him *immortal*! Can you believe that? Here was a man, understand, who had had more women than some of you have had hot dinners – to whom women actually *were* hot dinners, to be gobbled up and forgotten – and yet this was palpably no fake. When it came to detecting fake, believe me, I was a positive Geiger counter: this read *Real*. Congress with his sister – the sanctified encounter of the ancients – was actually going to release the Bull from our common condition, yours and mine! Strip off him like some chrysalis Time and the despair Time brings, and leave him free – *free*, my dears, in the only sense that finally matters. Without ageing. Without grief or physical pain. And *for ever*! Can you believe it? (*Pointing furiously*) *Him? . . . That?* . . . A randy, pseudo-intellectual, nearly mindless dummy dressed up as a prince!

AMNON: (*Smugly*) I have been Chosen, Yonadab. Think of it . . . You are looking at a Chosen Being. And you will benefit too.

YONADAB: I will?

AMNON: I know it absolutely. Companions of Immortals can also be immortal. Didn't you tell me the Egyptians believe this about their Pharaohs?

YONADAB: (*To audience*) That was actually true. They did. I did my best to look immensely flattered.

AMNON: What do you say?

YONADAB: I am immensely flattered.

AMNON: You think I'm mad?

YONADAB: Far from it. I did suspect it might be true, remember.

AMNON: You did!

YONADAB: Tell me – are you afraid?

AMNON: Why should I be? This is a sacred passion. I'm in the hands of Gods!

YONADAB: Of course.

AMNON: The only thing now is for you to keep your promise and assist them.

YONADAB: You mean bring her here.

AMNON: Exactly. Have you thought of a way?

YONADAB: Of course.

AMNON: You have?!

YONADAB: Naturally. I always mean what I say.

AMNON: (*Joyfully*) I think you're the most wonderful friend a man ever had! Ever, since the Day of Creation! I shall declare that publicly when I'm King.

YONADAB: I assure you I'm not worthy of that.

AMNON: You are – and much more! Much, much more! . . . (*Practically*) How will you do it?

YONADAB: The King is the only one who can let her out.

AMNON: So?

YONADAB: Send him word you're sick unto death. You haven't been to court for a week – that'll lend colour. He'll rush here to see you. Then ask him directly to let Tamar come and nurse you.

AMNON: He'll refuse.

YONADAB: Why?

AMNON: He likes refusing.

YONADAB: He'll be moved by your request. He'll find it humble and filial.

AMNON: It's stupid. That can't possibly work.

YONADAB: Why not?

AMNON: It's much too simple.

YONADAB: You want it difficult? Look, tonight she could be here with you, in your arms – your *destiny*!

(*He puts his arms around* AMNON*'s shoulders and speaks intimately.*)

You must woo her gently, Amnon. *Gently*. You must be as gentle with her as you mean to be with Israel. Make a covenant with her upon your bed, in love. In the name of Perpetual Peace.

AMNON: (*Sighing*) Ah . . .

YONADAB: (*To audience*) As I talked to him I knew one thing. *I had to watch.* Hidden somewhere – in some alcove – I had to see this for myself! How to manage it? It would be hard . . .

(*Suddenly* AMNON*'s sighs turn to groans.*)

AMNON: Ah! Ah!!

(*He doubles over.*)

YONADAB: What is it?

AMNON: (*Beginning to writhe*) Ah! Ahhh!

YONADAB: Amnon! What is it? Tell me!

AMNON: (*Shouting*) Help me here! Help me!

YONADAB: (*Calling also*) Help! You people – help your Master! (*Clapping*) Help the Prince Amnon!

(*Two* HELPERS, *now* BONDSMEN, *rush in as* AMNON *continues to groan and writhe.*)

AMNON: Bed! Get me to bed! Quick! Ahhh!

(*They support him; the group freezes.*)

YONADAB: (*To audience*) Incredible. Absolutely incredible. Within ten minutes of my suggesting it, he actually became ill. I mean violently. Again – no fake! Cramps – shakes – vomits – rivers of sweat staining his great bed. The whole repellent works.

(*The other* HELPERS *return bearing and strewing a great pile of coloured cushions, which they make up ceremoniously into a bed. The canopy above descends closer, to frame it. The two* BONDSMEN *lay their master on the cushions and cover him.*)

AMNON: Let me die! Let me die, O God! Kill me! Strike me to death! Kill me!
(*He rips off his amulet and hurls it away.*)
YONADAB: (*To the* BONDSMEN) Send for the King. Hurry!
(*The two* BONDSMEN *scuttle off.*)

SCENE SIX

Amnon's bedroom.

Light change. One of the remaining BONDSMEN *attempts to soothe* AMNON. *Another runs off and returns with a tray of bottles, and a bowl of water with a cloth. He wipes the feverish man's brow.*

AMNON: (*Writhing and babbling*) O God! O God of Israel! I have sinned! I am beyond pardon! Kill me! Break me into death! *Strike me!* Kill me! Kill me, O God, O God!
(*He falls back exhausted.*)
YONADAB: (*To audience*) Most of this, of course, was sheer terror of what he was about to do. Of two Fathers about to be abused – the One Above and the almost as frightening one below.
(DAVID *rushes in, followed by* ABSALOM, *Amnon's* BONDSMEN *and a* PRIEST, *holding a prayer shawl and the Saniph – the Royal Turban, on the front of which is a gold flower engraved in Hebrew with the phrase 'Consecrated to Yaveh'.*)
DAVID: Amnon! What is it? What has happened? (*To* YONADAB) Speak – you.
YONADAB: I don't know. It was so sudden –
DAVID: Is he poisoned? Was any food sent him?
YONADAB: No, Lord King.
DAVID: (*Seeing the Sign against Demons painted on* AMNON*'s chest*) What is this? Who put this on him? *You?*
YONADAB: (*Frightened*) No, Lord King!
DAVID: Then who?
YONADAB: I don't know – I imagine – He – he himself . . . To help himself . . .

DAVID: There is no help but from God who is One.
YONADAB: Of course, Lord King.
AMNON: (*Faintly*) I am found out.
DAVID: What? What does he say? (*He goes to him.*) Speak, my boy – let me hear you.
AMNON: I am found out. My foulness is found out . . .
DAVID: What do you mean, Amnon?
YONADAB: He's raving. He's far from himself.
DAVID: (*Silencing him*) Tssss! Tell me your heart, Amnon.
AMNON: I am foul, Father. There is foulness in me.
DAVID: (*Gently*) No, no. The foulness is *here*, my boy. In me!
AMNON: In *me*, Father. I swear it!
DAVID: Hush you! This is a rebuke to *me*: I know it! Over and over these past days when you stayed away I said to the court, 'He's drinking! He's whoring!' And all the time you were lying in pain. So am I punished for injustice!
AMNON: I am *wicked*, Father! This is the *truth*!
DAVID: No! You are *good*! You keep yourself from me *rightly* – because I am unworthy to have good children! But I will heal you. I will heal my Bull boy. The Lord of Mercy will hear my prayer and make you whole. You will see now! He will not afflict you for *my* sins. Absalom, robe me.

(ABSALOM *takes the prayer shawl from the* PRIEST *and robes his father. He takes the Saniph and places it on the King's head.*)

Now bow yourselves all and pray with me! Make his health your whole desire.

(*All on stage prostrate themselves.*)

YONADAB: And down they went in a transport of faith. And up went his head to God. And suddenly I felt in myself the longing that often came when I watched him pray: to enter his Believer's skull.

(*A low chord sounds.*)

DAVID: King of the Universe, we implore Thee!

(*All on stage groan.*)

Turn away thy wrath from this guiltless son and his unworthy father.

(*Groan.*)

Shine thy countenance upon us both and grant us joy.

(*All hum. Sotto voce.*)

YONADAB: (*Standing up and going near him*) Either this man is addressing nothing – or else there is a Court of Heaven. Either he is truly as self-deceiving as his son, or else he is a spokesman in that Court for himself – and *me* . . . In those few minutes, lying on the dusty rugs, I tried with all my being to imagine myself David – a Priest King influencing the universe. What must it be like to launch a massive appeal to the Unknown? To send out to It what also must be unknown to me – I mean my very *Self*: the Self of Myself without reservation? To let that be known by the vaster Unknown, and then returned to me with such tremendous force that I *can* know it – in the storming of my blood. Unknowable God confirmed as surely as the existence of myself! *Oh*, the wonder of that! To be Its entire resounding instrument! Not myself – yet never more myself!

DAVID: Selah.

YONADAB: Is it something like this?

DAVID: (*Dropping his arms*) The blessing of Him who is All be on you, Amnon, my son. May He give you life!

YONADAB: And look – He does! Or something does!

(AMNON *sits slowly up and extends his arms to his father.*)

AMNON: Father!

YONADAB: (*Resuming his position on the floor*) He is restored – as if rinsed clean of poison!

AMNON: Great Father! Ah!

DAVID: Tonight he will be himself again. (*To* AMNON) Sleep now. Rest all the day.

AMNON: One favour, I beg. If it is possible.

DAVID: All is possible for *you*! Name it.

AMNON: If it pleases you – let my sister come.

DAVID: *Tamar*?

AMNON: If she could stay by my side one hour – it would help me. She is good. I need goodness now – to give me strength.

(DAVID *looks away.*)

Are you angry? Forgive me – I have fever. Forgive the fever!

(*A pause.*)

DAVID: (*Fondly*) It is true. She is a healer, no doubt of it. When I was sick she prepared cakes for me with her own hands. She said simply, 'Eat these and be well!' – and as you know, I *was*! Yes! (*Pause.*) Why not? *Why not?* So be it! Let Tamar come here tonight. It's good.

ABSALOM: (*Springing up*) No!

DAVID: What?

ABSALOM: She must not! Should not! –

(*He stops, confused.*)

DAVID: Why?

ABSALOM: She has never been out from the palace – ever!

DAVID: So let her start. A first adventure.

ABSALOM: All the same . . . I do not think it good.

DAVID: You? *You* do not . . . *You?* Do you say, 'Nay' when I say, 'So be it'?

ABSALOM: (*Low*) No.

DAVID: (*Harsh*) What?

ABSALOM: (*Louder*) No, Beloved Father . . . Never.

DAVID: (*Staring into his face*) I hope not, Absalom. Not even in your heart.

(*He hands him the Saniph.*)

(*To* AMNON) She will come tonight, your sister, and do you ease. (*To* YONADAB, *sharply*) You now – wipe that foolishness from him!

YONADAB: Certainly, Lord King.

DAVID: (*Contemplating him*) Yonadab. The Man of Eyes.

YONADAB: I don't understand. Forgive me.

DAVID: (*To the others*) Come. Let's leave him. (*To* AMNON, *tenderly*) My Bull – that's who I want to see – strong again. Stamping his hoofs in my pasture – eh? Eh?

(*He prods jovially at the genitals of the sick man and sweeps out. The* PRIEST *goes with him.* ABSALOM *lingers, holding the Saniph.*)

ABSALOM: Our father has cured you, it seems.

AMNON: His powers have no limit.

ABSALOM: I will call again tomorrow.

AMNON: No! . . . I will rest tomorrow.

ABSALOM: As you please. (*To* YONADAB) You take the greatest care of my sister, when she comes.

YONADAB: Can you doubt it, Prince?

(ABSALOM *stares hard at both* YONADAB *and* AMNON.)

(*To audience*) Unpleasant moment. What could he know? Was he just jealous – or could they see as deep as they seemed to, those Shiner's eyes?

ABSALOM: Care, Yonadab.

(*He goes out. All the* BONDSMEN *bow.* AMNON *claps his hands and dismisses them. They leave.* YONADAB *takes up the bowl of water and the cloth and during the following wipes the wizard's sign from* AMNON*'s chest.*)

YONADAB: (*Excited*) Well, didn't I tell you?

AMNON: What?

YONADAB: It worked. I told you it would.

AMNON: Please . . .

YONADAB: What's the matter?

AMNON: Don't speak to me now. I'm very tired. It's been a huge ordeal.

YONADAB: Yes, but it's over now. Tonight she'll be here!

AMNON: Please . . . Just sit by me like the friend you are – and watch over me. And don't sleep. I may need you. It's very important I have peace now.

YONADAB: Of course.

AMNON: Good fellow: that's what you are. There are very few one would trust to watch at a time like this. It's a mark of how I trust you.

YONADAB: I'm flattered.

AMNON: Now I'll sleep. You're a marvellous fellow, Yonadab – there's no doubt about that. Marvellous . . .

(*He settles down to sleep.* YONADAB *finishes wiping his chest.*)

YONADAB: (*To audience*) And off he went – delighted with himself. Serene as a baby.

(*The light changes. A threatening music begins faintly.*)

Not so I. As the afternoon blazed and buzzed I grew more and more alarmed. Was this actually going to happen? In a few short hours she would be here – *in this room*! Surely Yaveh must show His hand now and stop it! How far would He let it go? – and what would His punishment be?

(*The sun glows red. The music grows louder and more sinister.*

ABSALOM *appears with the four* HELPERS. *He points dramatically at* YONADAB *in contemptuous denunciation, and in terrible slow motion the figures perform the Prince's bidding – miming the action described by* YONADAB, *although without actually picking him up physically*.)

(*During this*) And then a dizziness overcame me. I slipped down into a horrible dream. I saw Absalom wild-eyed, with a sword of judgment in his hand pointing straight at me! Around him his guards – bullies to a man. At a sign they surrounded me and carried me struggling towards a great door, opening into the street. And then they lifted me up high and hurled me into the gutter! Beggars were jeering all round me – dogs snapping at my thighs!

(*The sound of laughter echoes around the theatre*.)

And all the while a great voice clanged out in my head!

(ABSALOM *in mime opens his mouth wide. A voice calls out in the theatre:*)

VOICE: JUSTICE! JUSTICE! JUSTICE! . . . *JUSTICE!!*

(YONADAB *wakes with a cry. He also wakes* AMNON *with it*.

Light change.)

AMNON: What?

(ABSALOM *and the* HELPERS *leave the stage, in slow motion*.)

Is it late?

YONADAB: I don't know . . .

AMNON: I told you to watch over me, not sleep.

YONADAB: I know . . .

AMNON: What's the matter?

YONADAB: Nothing. I'm fine. Perfect. Marvellous . . . Never better.

AMNON: You're scared. I don't like that. It fills the room with wrong feelings.

YONADAB: Forgive me.

AMNON: You have to be calm, Yonadab. Look at me. I'm calm. I've been given the calmest sleep a man could have. Isn't that a Sign? Look outside – everything's calm there. Heaven is smiling. Only you are out of place.

YONADAB: A familiar situation.

AMNON: Well, change it. Summon my bondsmen. I have no strength in my hands as yet.

YONADAB: Of course.

AMNON: Tell them to bring new raiment. Purest white!

YONADAB: (*Clapping his hands and calling*) Raiment quickly for His Highness! Pure white!

AMNON: (*Calling too*) And hurry! (*To* YONADAB) I'm not blaming you. This calls for high courage. Not everyone has it.

YONADAB: (*Humbly*) Thank you.

AMNON: I shall sit at the window now. The departing sun is healthful, I believe.

(*The two* BONDSMEN *appear, carrying between them a white robe.*)

Ah. Enter. I am recovered, praise be to the King. Get me up and dress me.

(*They get him up and clothe him.*)

(*To them*) This evening my sister is coming. Tell the household I shall not be needing them again tonight. You two either. Admit the Princess, then go to your quarters. I do not wish to see a servant till dawn. Am I heard?

(*They bow.*)

Good. Now go.

(*They retire, taking the basin.* AMNON *crosses and sits by the 'window'.*)

(*To* YONADAB) Your face is still clouded, my friend.

YONADAB: Perhaps I have the sickness you had earlier.

AMNON: Impossible. That was a royal affliction, unavailable to commoners.

YONADAB: Forgive me again. Whatever was I thinking of?

AMNON: You make light of things too easily. I was being *searched*, don't you realize that? I was in the hands of Gods. I could actually feel their fingers in my entrails. Fetch me some perfume. And sprinkle some on the bed.

(YONADAB *fetches a stone bottle from the tray and sprinkles the bed.*)

What is really the matter with you? Be honest. Are you jealous?

YONADAB: Who wouldn't be? After tonight you'll be in

possession of a vast secret. You're about to experience something unimaginable – and all I can do is look on.

AMNON: (*Smugly*) I understand.

(YONADAB *goes to* AMNON *and pours perfume out of the bottle on to his head, then rubs it into the scalp and neck.*)

YONADAB: Tell me – would you – if I was discreet – permit me that?

AMNON: What?

YONADAB: To look on.

AMNON: You mean – *watch*?

YONADAB: I don't mean for pleasure. That of course would be abominable. What is about to happen will change you for ever. (*He rubs the perfume on to* AMNON*'s legs.*) I beg you let me be a witness. To share – as common men can only share – in the glory of royal ones.

AMNON: This is a holy act, Yonadab. It is between her and me, alone. Surely that is obvious.

YONADAB: Of course. I only asked . . . (*To audience*) Condescending prick.

AMNON: Actually I think you had better leave now, before she comes. She doesn't like you. It might well put her out to find you here. After tonight, of course, she will change. She will learn kindness. She will no longer be a little girl. And she will love all people. We both will.

YONADAB: Yes.

AMNON: Don't be offended.

YONADAB: I'm not, not at all. (*To audience*) There had to be a way to work it – but *how*?

AMNON: We have to make these journeys alone, you know.

YONADAB: Of course. I'm a crass man under everything, I'm afraid. I'm not really suitable to keep Princes company.

AMNON: Nonsense! You're the best friend a man ever had – ever, since the Day of Creation! Goodbye now. Wish your greatest wish for me.

(*Pause.*)

YONADAB: (*With 'profound' emotion*) Immortality!

AMNON: (*Moved*) Thank you . . . Thank you – dear fellow!

(*He clasps his hands fervently. At the same moment we hear the cry of porters filling the theatre, and growing louder: 'Way! Way! Way!')*

What's that?

(*Four* HELPERS *enter as porters, carrying a curtained litter. Beside it walks* MICAH. *The litter is set down.*)

YONADAB: (*Looking out of the 'window'*) She's come.

AMNON: No!

YONADAB: See for yourself.

AMNON: (*Standing up hastily*) But she's much too early. I'm not prepared! And who's that?

YONADAB: Her waiting-lady, I presume.

AMNON: No!

YONADAB: It has to be.

AMNON: No, no, no! – that can't be! I thought she'd come alone. I never thought – *You* never thought of that, did you?

(TAMAR, *veiled, appears out of the litter.*)

What shall we do now? *What on earth do we do?*

YONADAB: I don't know!

AMNON: Oh, wonderful! Wonderful! Yonadab the Planner! (*Bitterly*) 'The simplest plans are best, Amnon!'

YONADAB: Please lower your voice.

AMNON: Why? What's it matter? It's all impossible! *Impossible now!*

YONADAB: Please! I beg you!

(*A* BONDSMAN *hastily enters the room and bows to* AMNON.)

AMNON: (*Testily*) Yes, yes – I know! The Princess has arrived! Tell her to come up alone. No one else. Understand me? No one else.

(*The* BONDSMAN *makes a gesture of amazement.*)

YONADAB: (*Intervening*) Excuse me. (*To* BONDSMAN, *soothingly*) Ask the Princess to be so good as to honour us up here, *with* her attendants. Thank you.

(*The* BONDSMAN *bows, leaves the inner stage, crosses to the Princess and invites her to enter. The* PORTERS *unload dishes of fruit and flour from inside the litter.*)

(*To* AMNON) Please try to control yourself.

AMNON: For what? It's all ruined anyway!

YONADAB: Nothing is ruined.

AMNON: (*Suddenly shouting*) Of course it is! You haven't thought this out *at all*!

(TAMAR *and* MICAH *can clearly hear this row as they approach the house with the* PORTERS *bearing dishes*.)

YONADAB: Nothing is ruined, Amnon. Simply get a hold of yourself – or it will be!

AMNON: Get rid of her, do you understand? It's *your* plan, so you see it works!

YONADAB: I'll do my best.

AMNON: No! Do it! Not best – I don't want best! If that maid isn't out of here immediately I'll make you sorry! I'll make you the sorriest man in Israel, am I heard? Am I heard, damn you?!

(*The* BONDSMAN *shows* TAMAR *in to the inner stage, together with* MICAH *and the* PORTERS. MICAH *bows to the Prince and* YONADAB – *then unveils the Princess.* TAMAR *is exquisitely made up*.)

TAMAR: (*Coolly*) Why are you shouting? I thought you were sick.

AMNON: I am. Yonadab was baiting me.

TAMAR: How clever of him. What's he doing here anyway?

YONADAB: I was looking after the Prince.

TAMAR: (*Cold*) Yes? Well, there's no need to do that now. I'm here. You can go. (*To* AMNON) And why are you off your bed? Get back on it at once. *Go on!*

(*She claps imperiously.* AMNON *moves to his cushions, acting feeble*.)

(*To* YONADAB) How you could have let him stand, I cannot comprehend.

YONADAB: Members of your family tend to be wilful, Princess.

TAMAR: (*To* AMNON) Cover yourself – quickly! (*To* YONADAB) Believe me, I'll tell the King how you looked after him! He'll be interested.

(YONADAB *bows humbly*.)

(*Soothingly*) Never mind, Amnon. You're soon going to be well. I'm going to make you my special pancakes. They cured Father, and he was *really* sick. (*To* YONADAB) Where's the kitchen?

YONADAB: Through there, Princess.

TAMAR: Show the servants the way, and heat the vessels.

YONADAB: (*Coldly, to* BONDSMAN) Show the servants the way, would you?

(*The* BONDSMAN *snaps his fingers at the* PORTERS, *and they follow him out.*)

TAMAR: (*To* MICAH) You go in there too. Mix the batter.

AMNON: No – she mustn't stay!

TAMAR: Why not?

AMNON: I don't want her.

TAMAR: Of course she must stay. She's Micah. She's here to help me. Do you think I'm going to mix batter myself? That's servants' work! (*To* MICAH) Go in.

AMNON: No, Tamar. I was promised!

TAMAR: It's all arranged. Micah makes the cakes. I drop in the quince. With my own fingers. That's enough!

YONADAB: (*Creamily*) A thousand excuses, Princess – but it was the particular wish of your father that you serve the Prince without a maid.

TAMAR: Well, it's my particular wish that she stays.

YONADAB: Then with all humility I will have to inform the King he was disobeyed.

TAMAR: *What?*

YONADAB: I consider it my duty. I would urgently suggest that I take this lady back to the palace. Your Highness should not really incur your father's rage in this. Or you either, Madam.

MICAH: I don't understand. It is so absolutely unlike him, to order such a thing.

YONADAB: Nevertheless, he did; did he not, Prince?

AMNON: Absolutely. No question.

YONADAB: The Prince has a royal affliction in your father's view, which only another person of royal blood can cure – working alone. No common person should be present.

TAMAR: (*Flattered*) Oh . . . I see . . . Well, that does make a little difference.

MICAH: All the same, Madam, I cannot leave you. That would not be proper.

TAMAR: The King apparently wishes it.

MICAH: All the same I couldn't do it.

TAMAR: What?

MICAH: It would not be proper, Madam.

TAMAR: To obey the King's order?

MICAH: To leave you alone. I could not possibly do that. It's unheard of!

TAMAR: You'll go at once. That is my will.

MICAH: Madam – I dare not.

TAMAR: At once, Micah – Am I heard?

MICAH: Madam, I cannot . . . I will not do this, Madam! No!

(TAMAR *slaps* MICAH*'s face violently.*)

TAMAR: (*To* YONADAB) Take her to the palace immediately.

YONADAB: Willingly.

(YONADAB *claps; the* BONDSMAN *appears.*)

(*To him*) Princess Tamar's woman is leaving. Tell the porters.

(*The* BONDSMAN *bows and goes.*)

I wish Your Highness all return of strength. And a delicious supper. Princess, I envy him. (*To* MICAH) Come.

(*The two* PORTERS *come in from the 'kitchen'.* YONADAB *leaves, taking the perfume bottle with him.* MICAH *follows with the* PORTERS *into the 'street'.*)

(*To audience*) During this time, of course, I had worked out precisely how I could get to watch.

(*They walk round the stage down to the front.*)

TAMAR: I'll manage with just your servants. It'll be fun, for once.

AMNON: Not even with them, Tamar. Father said no one. Send them in here.

TAMAR: But that's absurd. I can't have *no* one!

AMNON: We must obey him. Remember what he always says: Those who rule must first learn to serve.

TAMAR: I hate this! What am I supposed to do – actually *cook* myself?

(*She marches off into the 'kitchen'.* AMNON *stares after her desperately. The lights go down more: the sun sets. The* PORTERS *stand by the litter.*)

YONADAB: Dear lady, I regret the Princess's temper.

MICAH: It's no matter.

YONADAB: I assure you no harm will come to her.

MICAH: I hope not, indeed.

YONADAB: If you could possibly accept this little gift to soothe your poor cheek, I would feel better. It is Prince Amnon's own perfume.

MICAH: I couldn't possibly, my lord.

YONADAB: A lady as charming as you deserves it. Please.

MICAH: Well, that's most kind.

YONADAB: (*Putting the bottle into her hand*) And if you will now excuse me, I regret I have the most demanding family business to attend to. If you could possibly consent to return to the palace on your own, you would do me the utmost of favours.

MICAH: Of course, my lord.

YONADAB: How *gracious* you are! Micah, isn't it?

MICAH: Yes, my lord!

YONADAB: Gracious Micah – goodbye.

(*He bows and leaves her. She gets into the litter and is borne off. He waves after her courteously and she returns the salutation. In the bedroom two* BONDSMEN *enter with flaming torches and place them on either side of the bed.*)

AMNON: Go to your quarters now and stay there. On pain of death. Am I heard?

(*They bow. He claps. They go out, crossing the outer stage.* YONADAB *dodges back on to the inner stage and takes up his position in a corner of it.*)

YONADAB: (*To audience*) I watched the servants cross the yard to their own quarters – and then, of course, I simply slipped back into the house and up the stairs. I had decided exactly where to hide. Between the bedroom and the ante-chamber was an internal window – the space of it filled with a huge stone vase of pine branches to freshen the air. Behind this I took up my station, totally concealed. And here I stayed all night without moving. Yonadab, your Special Correspondent. What follows was seen by nobody but me. Which makes you some of the most privileged viewers in the history of royal scandal.

SCENE SEVEN

YONADAB: What happened first was a smell. Vapour of olive oil from a pan: grated figs mixed with honey and coriander. It made me ravenous. He of course was well beyond that kind of hunger.

(AMNON *groans on his bed.*)

And then a sound: a sizzle as each pancake was dropped into the pan and flavoured with a spoonful of the sweet mixture at the soft hands of the girl.

(AMNON *groans louder.*)

AMNON: Tamar!

YONADAB: (*To audience*) Sizzle and smell and song . . .

AMNON: Oh!!

YONADAB: Sizzle and smell and song . . .

AMNON: Tamar . . . (*Suddenly shouting it out*) *Tamar!*

(*The song stops. The girl appears.*)

TAMAR: What is it? Are you in pain?

AMNON: Yes . . . No . . . Yes, I am . . .

TAMAR: You'll have to be patient. I haven't finished.

AMNON: I don't want anything to eat. Just sit by me. Here . . .

TAMAR: I've got to finish first.

AMNON: That's not important. Did you strike that woman on purpose?

TAMAR: What do you mean?

AMNON: To make her go.

TAMAR: Why should I do that?

AMNON: It's amazing . . .

TAMAR: What is?

AMNON: To be you . . . To be you!

(*He laughs uneasily.*)

TAMAR: I'm going to fetch the cakes.

AMNON: No!

TAMAR: They'll be spoilt if I don't!

AMNON: (*Touching her wrist softly*) After tonight you won't strike anyone again. You won't need to.

TAMAR: That's silly. There's nothing wrong in punishing a slave if she deserves it.

AMNON: You don't know what I'm saying. Tonight everything changes – and you don't know anything.

TAMAR: Changes?

AMNON: Tomorrow it will all be different. Not to be even imagined . . . We have to be taught – both of us. I as well as you.

TAMAR: Taught?

(*He draws her down gently to sit beside him.*)

AMNON: What is that on your eyes?

TAMAR: Malachite. Do you like it?

AMNON: When you were born Father gave you two priceless jewels to wear for life. Now I see that they are Signs.

TAMAR: My eyes?

AMNON: The body can have Signs – if it's pure enough. Did you know that? I have none. But you might give me some.

TAMAR: I don't know what you're saying.

AMNON: The Gracious shall give the Graceless grace! That's a prophecy.

TAMAR: I think you're a bit silly today.

AMNON: (*Touching her eyes*) If I died, would you weep those out of your head for me?

TAMAR: Of course.

AMNON: If you died, I'd weep mine out.

TAMAR: I wouldn't want them. They're too red.

AMNON: That's my sickness: you should pity me.

TAMAR: It's having women. Everyone knows that.

AMNON: Do you know what that means – to have women?

TAMAR: Of course I do. I'm not a child. (*Standing up*) Now I'm going to pray for you.

AMNON: What?

TAMAR: I've learnt the Prayer for the Sick, especially. I'm going to say it over you, and then you are going to eat.

AMNON: No, Tamar.

TAMAR: But yes! Now lie still. You think we're taught nothing in the harem, don't you? We are more devout than you, I can tell you that.

AMNON: I'm sure you are.

TAMAR: Don't laugh at me. I've heard how bad you are. Close your eyes. Now listen: hard. (*She adopts an attitude of prayer. Her voice is fervent and sincere.*) 'Blessed art Thou, King of the Universe, who giveth sickness and taketh it away. Relieve thy servant of his affliction. Quicken his being and restore his spirit for thy Name's sake. Amen.'

(AMNON *has sat up stealthily and is gazing at her.*)

'Selah.'

AMNON: You look amazing . . . Like Father . . . You have the same eyes when you pray.

TAMAR: (*Shocked*) Tsss!

AMNON: It's true. If we lived in Egypt I would have a huge statue carved of you doing that.

TAMAR: Tssss!

AMNON: I'd set it up in the desert for all to see.

TAMAR: Stop it. You know that's forbidden.

AMNON: Those eyes staring for miles – sparkling with chips of crystal. Men would travel for miles over the sand to see them. Tamar the praying statue! One of the wonders of the world! . . . They'd fall down before you.

(*She giggles, flattered.*)

They'd kiss your feet. Beautiful little veined feet – except they'd be huge. Each nail the size of an egg. In Egypt everything is colossal.

TAMAR: I hate Egypt.

AMNON: Why?

TAMAR: Because it afflicted us.

AMNON: Everyone afflicts everyone, Tamar . . . Except us. We'll be different.

TAMAR: Will we?

AMNON: Oh yes. We're born to it. To be gentle. Together!

(*He touches her foot.*)

I'll give you a riddle. They shall rise in peace before the people who first lie in peace unseen! Can you solve it?

TAMAR: No.

AMNON: Are you sure?

TAMAR: I don't understand!

AMNON: Don't you know the name of my sickness? Surely you know. You must feel something. You have to! You were chosen to choose me – you must feel something. When you came here – into here (*his head*) – you must have felt something!

(TAMAR *kicks away her foot, suddenly alarmed.* AMNON *rises to a kneeling position.*)

What's the matter?

TAMAR: Nothing.

AMNON: Sing to me.

TAMAR: Sing?

AMNON: Your song. You know which one . . . Please.

TAMAR: I don't remember it.

AMNON: You do. You know you do. (*He snaps his fingers and tries to laugh lightly, singing the melody.*) Hi-la. Hi-la. Hi-LA! *Sing! Please!*

(*A little scared now, the girl begins to sing.*)

That's it. Yes! Yes! But snap – you have to snap. *Snap!*

(*She starts to snap her fingers and dance tentatively.* AMNON *encourages her.*)

Yes! That's right . . . That's right . . . Their music . . . *Theirs!* Their song! They are singing *for us*!

(*She stops, staring at him in panic.*)

Don't be frightened.

TAMAR: (*Faintly*) I'm not!

(*He gets up off the bed, wildly excited.*)

AMNON: We're in their hands! They want it. It's ordained! You know what that means? *Ordered!* Even if we wished not to – we'd have to! They need us, Tamar. They – *need* us. You never thought Gods could need? But they do! They have to have *us*! That way they fulfil themselves on earth! (*More and more urgently*) We are to be their *companions*, Tamar – think of that! To rule in gentleness together – here on earth – to shed our love – shed it – shed it over all! And when we die, to be together always . . . You and I together always . . . Always . . . Amnon and Tamar – *Immortal!*

(*She gasps.*)

Yes! People will pray to *us* – that's what happens! *And we will be able to grant their prayers. Think of that!* 'I pray to Thee, Tamar! Amnon and Tamar – King and Queen – God and Goddess!'

(*Suddenly, the girl screams. He stops, startled.*)

TAMAR: (*Trying to control herself*) This is not you speaking, Amnon . . . It's – it's – it's a demon!

AMNON: No.

TAMAR: These aren't your words!

AMNON: They're not yours when you whisper.

TAMAR: What do you mean?

AMNON: (*Whispering*) 'I am yours, I am yours, Amnon! I'm here, Amnon. I'm with you! Amnon – Amnon – I'm yours!'

TAMAR: Stop it! *I don't know what you're saying! I don't know what you want!* I'm frightened . . . You're ill, and I'm frightened! I want to go!

AMNON: (*With supreme calm*) Come to me now. Don't speak any more. It's time now.

TAMAR: What for?

AMNON: No more words, Tamar. Just walk forward of your will. Say, 'I choose Thee!' That's all. And then silence. Come, gentle – gentle we will be! That's the way we must be. Gentle together.

(*He moves towards her. She moves away. They start to circle.*)

TAMAR: Amnon.

AMNON: Please.

TAMAR: Please, Amnon.

AMNON: Please now.

TAMAR: Amnon, please.

AMNON: Please.

TAMAR: Please, Amnon.

AMNON: Please . . . Please, Tamar . . . Please.

TAMAR: O God who created Heaven and earth, help me! O Lord who protectest Thy children, help me!

AMNON: No.

TAMAR: Thou art my shield – stretch forth Thy arm! O God, for Thy Name's sake, help me! (*In rapid earnest prayer*) For Thy Name's sake. For Thy glory's sake. For Thy mercy's sake. Thou alone art God, Thou One and Eternal – help me!

AMNON: Don't pray to Him! Come to me! Now!

TAMAR: O God Thou God O God Thou God! O God!

AMNON: (*In pain*) *You chose me, Tamar! Don't deny it any more! Tamar!*

(*A pause.*)

TAMAR: *Yes!*

AMNON: What?

TAMAR: It's true. I did.

AMNON: Ha?

TAMAR: I chose you. You found me out. I did it. Only – not now. It can't be now – this is wrong. We must go to Father: he'll help us. He'll change the law for us. Then we can do it openly. Everyone can see us love! Tomorrow we'll speak to him together – and everything you want will happen! Only let me go home tonight. Let's not soil it and make it bad.

YONADAB: (*Watching*) Clever girl.

TAMAR: If you love me, prove it. Let me go home now.

(*A pause.* AMNON *stands checked – head lowered like a bull – indecisive.*)

YONADAB: Don't run. Don't move at all. Just let it reach him.

TAMAR: Call the servants. Let them take me back. That way I'll know it's real – your love for me.

AMNON: (*Dully*) There are no servants. I sent them all away.

(*He raises his arms slowly towards her.*)

No one must witness this greatest thing.

(*He advances. Suddenly she breaks and tries to run past him, but he stops her lightly and tenderly.*)

Tsss! No one but us. Tamar and Amnon. Us.

TAMAR: (*Faintly*) No . . .

AMNON: Us . . .

TAMAR: Oh no . . .

AMNON: *Us!*

(*He folds her tightly in his arms. Hypnotized, she does not resist.*)

YONADAB: (*To audience*) For an age he held her there, clamped tight to him, sighing like the desert. Then slowly he raised the cage of his arms to let her out –

(*He does this.*)

– yet she stayed unmoving. Stillness absolute in her body.

Shock and wonder mingling . . . Then with hands of tender iron he lifted her. Like a priest with a sacred scroll he laid her for unwrapping on his altar. And with a reverence I had never even glimpsed in him before, he bowed himself down to her –

(*He lays her gently on the bed and kneels at the foot of it.*)

– saying aloud what she had only heard till then behind the grille of women praying.

AMNON: Holy! Holy! Holy!

(*He lowers his head to her feet. This brings her to herself. She scrambles away up the bed. Slowly he follows her over the cushions. Then, facing upstage, he suddenly tears off his robe.* TAMAR *stares at him.*)

TAMAR: I am Tamar. Look at me, Amnon. I am Tamar.

(*He looks at her.*)

AMNON: Thou art my sister, whom I love.

(*Now he stands, naked out of his clothes, his back to the audience. He reaches up to a string attached to the canopy.*)

YONADAB: And then, weirdly, with automatic gesture – as if compelled to it by some voice within – he stretched out his hand and slowly *pulled down the curtains in my face*!

(*The white curtains are released on their wooden rings. They fall in a great cascade and surround the bed.*)

(*Outraged*) Why? *Why??* I couldn't believe it! What had he to do with curtains? A bull with bed curtains? He never pulled curtains in his life, I'd swear to that! So why now at this one moment? (*Increasingly furious*) Damn! . . . Damn! Damn! Damn! Damnation! I wanted to rush in there and rip them down! This was all it had come to – all my planning – plots and plans for days, to come to this! *Curtains!* It was like some fantastic joke against me! Or some rebuke – (*Pause.*) Yes. But Who was doing the rebuking?

(*He looks upwards, struck with sudden alarm.* TAMAR *cries out from behind the curtain.*)

TAMAR: *Ah! . . . Amnon!*

AMNON: No, Tamar – no . . . No . . . (*Violently*) *You must!*

YONADAB: (*Upset*) *Oh no! No, no! Not! – I beg!* Not that! Not that!

(TAMAR *cries out again, louder.* YONADAB *claps his hands over his eyes.*)

Ah! I never wanted that, I swear! 'Gently,' I said. 'Be gentle!'

(*Music rises, menacing and savage. Shadows rise also in the torchlight of the curtains.*)

Yes, but this is it, Yonadab. This is what *is* – so *see* it! Look at it! Force yourself to see through the flickering light. You don't need flesh to understand: shadows will do! Look at *them*!

(*With increasing visibility the shadows of their bodies are thrown on to the curtain: immense black shapes enlarged and distorted by the lamps. During the following speech they make a series of abstract and strange shapes: a mysterious procession of glyphs.*)

(*To audience*) All my life I remembered what I saw that night: the shadows! – more terrible than bodies. The limbs thrown up on the curtains like the letters of some grotesque language formed long, long before writing. There on the fall of a Jerusalem drape I saw, writ enormous – like a parody of our Hebrew consonants – the archaic alphabet of the Book of Lust. I watched in horror as their bodies slipped and shaped – seemed to form words: the hoops and humps of a calligraphy capable in the end of just one sentence: *Despair* . . . Increasing, accumulating, annihilating, inescapable *Despair*. Look – look yourselves! Hoops of the hunted woman writhing! Humps of the hunting man riding! – round and round in the forest of his fury where all paths lead back to the same blank clearing! Shapes of hurting and being hurt. Hers finally exhausted – the rigour of acceptance like the rigour of death. His wilder and still wilder, still seeking to hurl himself through her to *freedom*. Seeking a bliss to end the need for bliss! Beyond and beyond his uttermost reach for ever!

(AMNON *cries out.*)

Which do you see there? Man bucking to touch a non-existent God? Or Man bobbing on a non-apparent string – held by the jerking hand of that very God: the oldest puppet show in the world? (*Softer, as the light dies slowly on the curtain*) Beyond. Beyond. Beyond. Beyond. Always beyond! Until at last the will dies. Or the string snaps. Whichever . . . And he falls senseless in the sealed dungeon of himself.

(AMNON *gives a terrible, lingering, agonized moan and his shadow falls downward on to the bed. Long pause.*)

(*Bitterly*) In other words – it was just another fuck!

(*The light changes abruptly to dawn.*)

His words – *his!* – hurled at her in the dawn. As if *he* were the one who had been assaulted!

AMNON: (*Shouting*) That's all! *That's all!*

(*He tears a curtain down with a rattle of wooden rings.* TAMAR *is revealed lying naked. The lamps have been extinguished.*)

Another fuck – that's all! If you *knew*! If you *knew*! You dare everything – everything! For what? (*Savagely*) What did you do? A spell, wasn't it? You spelled me! Confess! You put a spell on me in the damn harem – you witch! You damned witch – you witched me!

(*He pushes her violently; she does not move.*)

Get out! Quick – before I hurt you! What? Shall I call my men? They'll know how to treat you. You won't be the first whore they've thrown out of here! Witch-whore!

(*A pause. He stands panting and shaking. Slowly* TAMAR *gets off the bed. She picks up the curtain to cover herself.*)

TAMAR: (*Quietly*) What you are doing now is even worse than what you have done.

(AMNON *raises his arm to strike her – but remains paralysed, making guttural splutters of mad frustration. Finally he spits at her and runs out of the room, offstage.* TAMAR *stands alone. Elaborately she winds the curtain round herself so that it trails behind her like a parody of a wedding dress. Then she steps forward on to the outer stage. She freezes. The lights change, and the inner stage is dark. The canopy withdraws. A low chord sounds.*)

SCENE EIGHT

The streets of Jerusalem.

During the following scene the light very gradually brightens into day as TAMAR *walks with extreme slowness and deliberation around the outer space.* YONADAB *follows her at a distance.*

YONADAB: (*To audience*) Silently I follow her – down the stairs and out into the street: the harsh cold of earliest morning. Around her a vast labyrinth of streets: lanes, alleys, passageways running in all directions. She has never seen any of these before – she has never been out of the palace for a single day. And yet she moves through them unhesitatingly! – in a kind of trance of deliberation – as if she knows exactly where she is going! *How can this be?* I follow as if enclosed in one of my vivid dreams – watching her tiny figure, wound in its curtain like a mockery bride, moving in this fantastic certainty.

(*The music rises. They walk in slow motion.*)

On either side walls hem her in. The doors in them still shut, the windows fast sealed. On she moves – on – like a blind girl who sees inside her head the clearest goal, and makes towards it, undeterrable. On – on – on – and I behind her creeping like a spy, drawn by the thread of this almost unimaginable event. Suddenly she stops.

(*A structure representing a crenellated tower descends to hang above the inner stage.*)

I know exactly where she is – but she cannot. This is the house of Absalom, her adored brother, which she has never seen. It is almost as if some invisible hand has led her here to its very door. How frightening this whole event has become! An invisible hand seeming to draw curtains on which I must read a horror at the heart of congress. Now seeming to pull a girl helpless through a maze of streets . . . What now? Is she going to knock?

(TAMAR *throws back her head and opens her mouth: then shuts it.*)

No, worse: she's going to cry out! Summon the city! She's going to *tell* her shame! *Oh no!* No, no, no! (*To her*) Go home, Tamar. Quickly! Make some excuse – Amnon was too sick to leave – *anything!* But say nothing! What's real for you is marriage – a bearable future. You can still have them! Just don't speak. Go on. Go on – slip home now!

(*She kneels.*)

Fool: she's going to do it. With one sound ruin her life. *Oh these children of David! – these idealists!* Like her deluded brother she is going to make her own stab at the sublime – *at making things mean more than they do or ever can!*

(TAMAR *opens her mouth again.*)

(*Savagely*) Go on then – get on with it. No one can stop you – least of all Yonadab!

(*But she closes it again and mimes scooping up earth from the ground.*)

Ah no – ritual abasement first, of course! Dirt on the head – chicken droppings – the proper antique manner. Go on, do it all!

(*She mimes pouring dust on her head.*)

That's right. Now you're ready. Good. Go! Let's hear it. Pronounce the sentence on your own life – Spinsterhood for ever. *Go on! Do it!*

(*She gives a soft cry.*)

(*Pitiless*) Louder than that. We can't hear you! You're trying to fill the ages, aren't you? Make a Legend, no? That little squeak won't do it! Come on now – *loud!*

(*She cries louder. A* TOWNSMAN *appears and stares at her.*)

That's better. Again – louder! Louder still, please!

(*Her cry rises. A* TOWNSWOMAN *appears and stares at her.*)

Louder! We must never forget you, Tamar! Never, never, never!

TAMAR: (*Standing up and yelling*) AHHHHHHHHH!

YONADAB: That's it. That's it! Fill our ears with it! Tell it to the world!

(*Two more* TOWNSMEN *rush in and stand astounded. Her cry becomes utterance.*)

TAMAR: I am Tamar, daughter of the King. My brother Amnon has raped me and thrown me in the street.

(*A low gasp fills the auditorium.*)

I am Tamar, daughter of the King! My brother Amnon has raped me and thrown me in the street!

(*The gasp is repeated, louder. Two more* TOWNSMEN *appear and now in the auditorium we hear voices calling – 'What's that? What's she say?' – and fragments of her sentence repeated, as a crowd obviously assembles and reacts.* TAMAR *simply faces front and repeats the same sentence as the noise in the theatre grows in volume, and the* TOWNSPEOPLE *mime their shock and outrage. At the climax of this huge sound the sun appears and illumines behind her the inner stage: kneeling on it, half naked, as if awakened from sleep among the cushions, is* ABSALOM. *Slowly he rises and reaches for his cloak. All the voices of the unseen crowd cry, 'Absalom!' There is silence as their favourite steps off the inner stage. The* TOWNSPEOPLE *prostrate themselves. He walks forward to where his sister stands – staring at her in horror. He puts his cloak around her. A low murmur of approval. She falls into his arms.*)

ABSALOM: (*Grimly*) You shall have *Justice*! (*Shouting*) Selah!

(*The theatre fills with cries of 'Justice!' and 'Selah'. He leads her back on to the inner stage and then off.*)

YONADAB: (*To audience*) Ruin! Ruin to the House of David! And I the ruiner! Yonadab the family joke – Lord over them all! Lord over Him too above – *Yaveh the Non-God!* Hadn't I proved that now up to the hilt? If He lived I'd have been dead beyond anyone's doubt. So then – what followed? The whole Tribe was deluded! Lost in falsehood! Braying to *Nothing!* Yonadab the Destroyer was the Bringer of Truth!

(*Pause. He comes downstage in a cone of light. All the others leave the stage.*)

I should have been skipping like a mountain goat. But I wasn't. I felt no joy at all. Not the slightest wriggle of triumph. The scandal was coursing through the city – crashing at its foundations – and all I could hear was *one sound* from the preceding night. That cry of his.

(*Lights up on the inner stage where* AMNON *now stands frozen in the attitude we have already seen – his arm raised to strike, his mouth open in a silent yell.*)

That one cry of the Bull in the dawn of just another morning. That yell of emptiness. In my head it wouldn't stop.

(*The lights go slowly down as* AMNON *leaves the stage.*)
But why? What else had I expected? A pumping man, a wriggling woman and an empty world – that's all there is. I knew that. So then, what else had I thought could possibly occur? Why had I stayed all night? Because I *had*, you realize – six, seven hours with nothing to look at but a bed curtain! The dirtiest-minded of you would have left long before. Was it possible under everything that I had actually been kept rooted there by some kind of *hope*? The tiniest, faintest, absurdest tickle of hope that at the end of all those writhing, raunchy images I might behold *one new one* which could change my life? Had I stood there all that time – let me say it in all its idiocy – had I actually stayed to witness, between two dim-witted, super-ordinary people rutting themselves senseless in a Jerusalem night, what even you would call the most stupendous sight this world could ever offer: *The Birth of Godhead*? Yonadab the Cynic – sceptic, sneering Yonadab – a *sharer* in *Immortality*? (*He laughs.*) No: of course not. Even granted that grain of longing we all have in us for one irrefutable and redeeming wonder – *of course not!* Never in my knowing life could I have hoped for anything so totally impossible! Never.
(*Pause.*)
No. (*Pause.*) No. (*Pause.*) No. (*Pause.*) No. (*Pause.*) No.
(*Long pause. He regards the audience.*)
Yes.
(*Blackout.*)

ACT TWO

SCENE ONE

On the inner stage sits DAVID *enthroned, his prayer shawl on his head and drawn over his face.* ADONIJAH, ITHREAM, SHOBAB *and* SHEPATIAH *sit below him, scared.* ABSALOM *stands before him, defiant – his hand flung out in a frozen attitude of demand, flanked by his two* GUARDS *bearing their staves. Before the throne lies the bed curtain which* TAMAR *wore, lying where* ABSALOM *has cast it. On the outer stage down front, in much brighter light, stands* YONADAB.

YONADAB: (*To audience*) You know, this is really a story of demons. The Demon of Mischief who lives in the despised man. And the Demon of Credulity who lives in the Cynic. Both of them slept in me – and both woke. The first destroyed my friend: the second, myself. On that night when superstition reached its apex in the house of Amnon, it had arisen also in me. Deeply humiliating as this is to admit. Buried deep under the crust of my rational mind – which you must have noticed was in many ways far more ahead of its time than any of your minds are now of yours – there had surfaced a hope so *ir*rational I could not believe I could give it head room. Something was going to happen to make sense of my life by its very *non*-sense! Two quintessentially average figures would attain immortality – and spill it by proximity on to *me*! What sane man would consider for a second a thought so ludicrous – even living as I did in a world of primitive dark, where anything might be possible? When I realized exactly how deeply primitive I actually was – I was staggered. I was too honest to deny it – but I did my best to thrust it all back inside as hard as I could. Let the rest of the Tribe believe inanities – not me! Not Yonadab!
(*Pause.*)

Of course I knew exactly what attracted me to the fantasy – and, I think, so do you. If you could have your choice today, my dears – smart and modern dears as you are, festooned with your computers and your calculators – which would you finally rather witness? Men and women walking out into the sky on to further and further stars, filling the universe with more of *You* – or you walking here, but in another state of Being, freed from the conditions which enslave you now? A state in which you grew more wise, each day, not less. More filled with adoration, not less. In which you did not sicken, or watch others sicken. In which you did not illustrate your length of life leaking your excrement, repeating your venom, dribbling your jumbled memories before crumbling repetitions of yourselves – impaled in deepening depression on the unextractable point of Pointlessness. If you answer the second – then a little pity, please, for a desperate son of Palestine three thousand years ago, who hadn't even your advantages. And if you say to me, fine, all right, the fantasy is attractive, but how on earth could anyone have thought it remotely *possible*, or even *desirable*, with two people so totally third rate as the couple shown us – an over-sexed dummy and a petulant little prick-teaser? – I answer this: On whom else should a Divine Choosing fall? Surely no one here believes they could ever actually *deserve* Divinity? Do they? . . .
(*He waits for a reply.*)
Well then, the more average the undeserver, surely the better. The more muddled, greedy, vapid, vulgar and generally pathetic the better – because the more in need of change. The more like me. And you . . . Let's get on with the story.
(*Lights come up on to the inner stage.* YONADAB *steps on to it.*)

ABSALOM: (*Shouting*) Justice!

YONADAB: (*To audience*) Noon of the same day. Jerusalem seething. All I could think of now was the need to save my own skin.

ABSALOM: The Lord knows it is a dreadful thing to urge a brother's death. For the sake of our Law – which alone distinguishes us from beasts – and of Tamar, my sister – my dear, wronged sister – I demand that Amnon be put to death as the beast he is.

(*His* GUARD *bang their staves.*)

YONADAB: (*To audience*) He has actually been going on like this for one full hour. What can it feel like to be so noble? I myself am so contorted, straight-forwardness like his is almost an aphrodisiac.

ABSALOM: (*To the Princes*) *Am I heard?* Who will support me? Do I speak alone, brothers?

(*The four* PRINCES *hang their heads in embarrassed silence.*)

Who would believe this? Your sister never will when she is told. Why do you not speak?

(DAVID *coolly lowers his prayer shawl.*)

DAVID: Perhaps they are waiting for him whose duty it is.

YONADAB: (*To audience*) At last. He has been silent all this time. Which side of himself will he now deign to show us? The just or the vain? Alas for David.

DAVID: Tell me – and, if you can, in a manner more moderate – where is Tamar at this moment?

ABSALOM: In my house.

DAVID: Why did she not come to me?

ABSALOM: I found her in the street, and took her in.

DAVID: Why did she not come with you now?

ABSALOM: She preferred to stay within doors. Surely that is understandable.

DAVID: She does not think I am able to give her justice? I am too feeble to be her champion, is that it? Or simply too old, perhaps?

ABSALOM: Of course not!

DAVID: She *prefers* – I understand. She *prefers* to stay with you. I only gave her everything. Her lightest wish was a commandment laid on my heart. But she *prefers* to keep from me. Good. The most precious jewel – (*extravagantly indicating his sons*) the centre of my diadem of perfect jewels – *prefers* . . . Or did you suggest it? What did you say to her? 'The King is too weak to deal with this. I'll do it for him'?

ABSALOM: Never! May my eyes be sealed if I spoke one such word!

DAVID: So then she decided for herself. 'I'll seek out my hero brother! His brave young arm will be my shield. Let's not bother with the feeble King!'

ABSALOM: Great Father, on my head I swear to you: this is not how it happened. She *encountered* me. She did not seek me out!

DAVID: (*Suddenly exploding*) *She shamed me!* Before all people! *Shamed!* (*Pause.*) Today they will shoot their lips out as I pass. 'There's David our King, whom even girls ignore! Let him go back to sheep!'

ABSALOM: (*Exasperated*) She was embarrassed to come! I am amazed you cannot understand it.

DAVID: Sheep and goats! That's all he's fit for now! Goats and sheep! Baa! Baaa! Baaa!

ABSALOM: *You turn things round!* Always the same! It is *she* who is shamed – not you! You lose sight of real things!

DAVID: A fault with the old.

ABSALOM: Then let the young keep you on the track.

(*A murmur of horror goes up. Pause.*)

(*Retracting*) I abase myself before you, O King of Majesty.

DAVID: (*Ignoring this*) Oh go on, please.

ABSALOM: (*Collecting himself; angry*) Your wrong in this, Father, is nothing to hers. That is all I intended.

DAVID: And are you now a Judge in Israel?

ABSALOM: I'm a *man*! One does not have to be Priest–King to know iniquity.

(*All the* PRINCES *hiss in condemnation.*)

DAVID: You are intemperate today.

ABSALOM: Abomination has occurred today! I demand that the man be punished who has caused it. That is all! The Law must be fulfilled! That is your duty!

DAVID: (*Furious*) What?

ABSALOM: Why should any man in Israel obey it if you do not? A lawful King is a law-loving King. If you do not honour it – without favour – no one – no one need ever again – *ever again* –

DAVID: What? Need ever again – *what*?

ABSALOM: Honour *you*! Yes!

(*The* PRINCES *clap their hands over their mouths.*)

DAVID: I rule by love – not terror. But I rule. Not you.
(He steps over the bed curtain and grips ABSALOM *by the hand.)*
Amnon is my son, and I will decide his fate – alone. You will not touch a hair of his head. Swear that upon your own.
(Pause. Trembling, ABSALOM *touches his brow.)*
No – on your own *hair*!
*(*ABSALOM *touches his hair.)*

ABSALOM: I swear.
(Pause. DAVID *abruptly departs.)*
(To the PRINCES*)* But he will never sit upon the throne of Israel! – believe that! Nor you either – if that is in your minds. Tell your brothers that, who have avoided me today! Cowards! *Cowards! All of you!*
(The PRINCES *scuttle away after their father, taking the throne with them.* YONADAB *surreptitiously tries to make his exit too. He moves on to the outer stage.)*
(Calling after him) Yonadab.

YONADAB: *(Airily)* Yes, Prince?

ABSALOM: Come with me to my house.

YONADAB: I regret infinitely I cannot, just at this moment. Pressing family business.
*(*ABSALOM *claps sharply. His two* GUARDS *march downstage towards* YONADAB *and flank him on both sides, showing their sharp staves.)*
I imagine it is just possible to postpone it.
(He is marched back to the inner stage. At the same moment the crenellated tower descends to hang above it, and TAMAR *– veiled – appears behind* ABSALOM*. He turns and takes her tenderly by the hand. Light change.)*

SCENE TWO

Absalom's house.

TAMAR: *(Urgently)* What happened? What did he say?

ABSALOM: *(Embarrassed)* Keep private. I'll tell you later.

TAMAR: But what did he say? Tell me now!

(*He indicates* YONADAB. *She gasps on seeing him.*)

ABSALOM: Go in please. I will come to you.

TAMAR: But will he act? Tell me that at least! Will he do something – Father? . . . Did he speak of me?

ABSALOM: (*Exploding in anguish*) *Tamar!* This is not the time! Go in. I order you.

(*Frightened, she goes in.* ABSALOM *rounds on* YONADAB.)

So now. All of it.

YONADAB: What do you mean?

ABSALOM: Your part in this.

YONADAB: Mine?

ABSALOM: You were with Amnon last night.

YONADAB: I left when the Princess arrived. Ask the servants – they saw me go!

(ABSALOM *claps his hands. Two more armed* GUARDS *appear.*)

ABSALOM: The truth, Yonadab.

YONADAB: (*Frightened*) I told you. I left them together. He was sick. Your sister had come to help. That's all I know.

(ABSALOM *nods. A* GUARD *strikes* YONADAB, *pitching him on to the floor. He cries out.*)

ABSALOM: The truth, Yonadab.

YONADAB: That is the truth! Obviously it was all a stratagem, his sickness. I swear before God who is One, I knew absolutely nothing of what he purposed – *Ah!*

(*He is struck again.*)

I swear!

(*And again.*)

Stop it! Stop it! I'm an innocent man! Damn you! Stop!

(YONADAB *is beaten ferociously. Finally* ABSALOM *gives the signal to stop.*)

ABSALOM: (*Kneeling over him*) Make no mistake. I will know what happened. (*To the* GUARDS) Throw him in the street.

(ABSALOM *stalks offstage. The four* GUARDS *lift up* YONADAB, *using exactly the same gestures we have already witnessed in his dream – the same music sounding. They toss him on to the outer stage. The theatre is filled with the sound of a crowd jeering and hurling insults.* YONADAB *picks himself up, hobbles around the stage, terrified – ducking and weaving to escape thrown objects. Suddenly the light changes and the noise cuts off.*)

YONADAB: (*To audience*) I reached home as best I could – not before a good number of stones and donkey pats had found me. There were no bones broken, thank heaven – but the whole event was the most frightening, not to mention humiliating, I'd experienced in my whole life. Later I got very angry. I was, after all, a member of the Royal Household – no matter how inferior. To be thrown out among dogs and beggars was really beyond endurance!

(*Pause.*)

There was, however, one deeply weird thing about it. I'm sure you've noticed it already. Do you remember my dream about Absalom – before the rape? You might almost believe I had prophetic powers! If you weren't so clever and modern, that is. Even so, you must be a little impressed. It was virtually inexplicable, you have to admit. Sufficiently beyond rational explanation to be alarming. No?

(*The noise of the crowd rises again in the theatre, only fainter. The tower withdraws above the inner stage.* AMNON *creeps on to it carrying a jug of wine and a cup, and sprawls drunkenly and scared. The awning falls.*)

I remained indoors for a week, whilst the mob besieged Amnon's house. I could hear them even a mile away, moaning for a stoning – their universal solution to everything. Finally David sent soldiers from the palace to disperse them.

(SOLDIERS *march in and stand before Amnon's house with drawn swords.*)

Only then did I dare venture out to see my wretched friend.

(*He hobbles upstage to Amnon's house. The* SOLDIERS *admit him.*)

Exactly how wretched I could never have guessed.

SCENE THREE

Lights up on the drunken, quaking man.

YONADAB: Amnon? My dear?
AMNON: Hah?
YONADAB: How are you?
AMNON: (*Angry*) Where've you been?
YONADAB: At home.
AMNON: Hiding?
YONADAB: Of course.
AMNON: A *friend* would have come at once! How selfish you are!
YONADAB: I'm sorry – I had problems of my own. I was actually almost killed by your brother's men.
AMNON: I've been almost killed by half Jerusalem.
YONADAB: But your father protected you.
AMNON: For the moment.
YONADAB: If I were you I'd go to him right away. I'd throw myself flat at his feet in front of the whole court and refuse to get up till he forgave you. He'd have to do it. He needs you. Absalom is much too popular.
AMNON: I can't do that.
YONADAB: Why not? He'll thunder away at you for half an hour, then announce it's God's will you be forgiven. There's nothing to it.
AMNON: I can't do it, Yonadab! Anyway it doesn't matter. What I do or Father or anybody. It's all arranged.
YONADAB: What do you mean?
(AMNON *laughs.*)
AMNON: You're not really very clever, are you?
YONADAB: I do my best.
AMNON: Book-learning, that's all you're good for. You don't see what's before your face.
YONADAB: And what is that?
AMNON: It's all meant. Every bit of it. I'm just an instrument – and so are you.
YONADAB: I don't quite understand you.
AMNON: It's all *meant*, Yonadab . . . Foreseen! . . . The Ugly

Ones prepare the road: the Beauties walk on it!

YONADAB: Excuse me – as you say, I'm not very clever.

AMNON: (*Slyly*) Tell me – where are they at this moment, my beautiful brother and sister?

YONADAB: In his house.

AMNON: Doing what?

YONADAB: How should *I* know?

AMNON: They say no one sees them.

YONADAB: So?

AMNON: (*Mysteriously*) They're in the egg.

YONADAB: Egg?

AMNON: When it cracks open the birds will fly out. Like golden eagles. When they die they'll fly straight into Heaven.

YONADAB: Do you think you could try to explain yourself a little less poetically?

AMNON: It's been *them* all the time. Under our noses. We never saw it . . . They were always close – even as children. Always staring at each other in that secret way. I must have been mad to think it could have been me, looking like me. It's been *them* all the time.

YONADAB: Them *what*, for heaven's sake?

AMNON: Chosen, of course! Ordained – to be Gods!

YONADAB: (*Exasperated*) Oh, *no*!

AMNON: All the signs are there! Every one!

YONADAB: Oh no, Amnon – *please*!

AMNON: You think I'm just drunk?

YONADAB: I think I've had enough of nonsense – that's what I think! *All of it!* Gods! Choosings! Ordainings! I don't want to hear another word of this as long as I live.

AMNON: (*With calm assurance*) They have been chosen, Yonadab. Absalom and Tamar. I can prove it absolutely.

YONADAB: Good.

AMNON: I can show you all the Signs.

YONADAB: Wonderful.

AMNON: You'll believe me when you hear them! Will you listen?

YONADAB: No.

AMNON: I'll prove it to you beyond any doubt.

YONADAB: I want you to stop this. It's all *rubbish*, every bit of it!

Stuff for old women and village idiots! Let's forget we ever started it. Keep our mouths shut and heads down and hope it'll all go away!

AMNON: (*Insistently*) Listen to me! Listen! –

YONADAB: I don't want to!

AMNON: (*Crying out*) It's your *destiny*! You *have* to understand! *Please! It's yours as well!*

(*A pause.*)

YONADAB: (*Resigned*) Very well. What are they – these wondrous Signs?

(AMNON *adopts a 'prophetic' posture and freezes.*)

(*To audience*) And of course he told me. Three impressive, dumbfoundingly clear Signs that they had been chosen for Godhead, the Princess and the Shiner. In other words, a cataract of pure lunacy. You'll hear it all for yourselves in a few minutes. Just wait.

AMNON: There! . . . What do you think now?

YONADAB: That you've been in this room too long.

AMNON: They're not Signs?

YONADAB: They are nonsense – that's all. Now, once and for all, will you leave this alone?

(*Pause.*)

AMNON: I'm frightened, Yonny. I dream all the time.

YONADAB: (*Uncomfortably*) We all dream. I'm quite good at it myself.

AMNON: They come for me – Absalom and Tamar – hand in hand – wearing crowns! They tie me with a long rope here (*His fork*) and lead me through the streets! Light shines from their hands . . .

YONADAB: Amnon, please!

AMNON: The King will be powerless before them, you'll see. He'll flee from the city. They will rule in his stead. I know it absolutely! Absalom and Tamar – husband and wife!

YONADAB: (*Scared*) I'm going! This is too dangerous. Your servants must be listening to every word!

AMNON: You've got to go to him! To *Absalom*!

YONADAB: (*Startled*) Me?

AMNON: Be my Ambassador. Speak to him for me!

YONADAB: I've already been with Absalom, thank you. I didn't exactly relish the experience.

AMNON: I know he beat you, but that's good.

YONADAB: Indeed?

AMNON: Yes, because now *you* can forgive *him* – and then he can forgive *me*! Everyone forgives everyone! Tell him I'll do anything he wants. I'll – I'll kiss the girl's feet before his door. What about that? I'll lie on my face and his servant can piss on my head – how about that? Oh no, no, that's too much! But something. You tell me. You're deep at advice. What should I promise?

YONADAB: I can't begin to suggest.

AMNON: Why not say I am sick unto death from shame? I'm lying on my bed in agony and he should come and show me some pity.

YONADAB: Don't you think that particular story has been rather used up?

AMNON: (*Furious*) Then you tell me! Don't just sneer! *Yonadab the Sneerer!*

YONADAB: (*Also angry*) I don't *care*, Amnon! *I don't care any more!* I'm not going back there – and that's final!

(*Pause.*)

AMNON: (*Hard*) You *are*, my friend.

YONADAB: Yes? How will you make me?

AMNON: You go to him today – or I'll send word to him you helped me. And to the King.

(*Pause.*)

YONADAB: Will you indeed?

AMNON: I . . . didn't actually mean that.

YONADAB: Didn't you?

AMNON: Of course not! It was just a joke! You know how I joke! I'm asking you as a *friend*: that's all. The best friend a man ever had! You can't abandon me now. Look – please – I'm asking as one friend to another. Not a Prince – a friend. Yonadab . . . *Yonny* . . . Yonny Yonadab . . . the best friend a man ever had, since the Day of Creation . . .

(*Sloppily, he puts his arms round* YONADAB*'s legs.*)

YONADAB: Amnon, please . . .

AMNON: I'm begging, Yonny . . . I'm your mat . . . The carpet beneath your feet! Dust . . . I'm dust . . . That's all I am. (*Imploring*) PLEASE! (*As a child*) Please . . . Please . . . Please . . .

YONADAB: (*With distaste*) All right.

AMNON: You will?

YONADAB: I said so.

AMNON: Oh, bless you! Blessings on you, Yonadab! Blessings!

YONADAB: Goodbye.

(*He steps out on to the outer stage. The awning rises.* AMNON *staggers off to the side of the outer stage with his cup of wine and sits in dim light. The* SOLDIERS *leave.*)

(*To audience*) And for the last time I did his bidding. Anything to get away from him. Besides, it was worth trying, to ingratiate myself with Absalom. I needed a new protector – that was clear. This lump was no use any more. Bull had become ox. Shit-scared, I went back to that dangerous beauty.

SCENE FOUR

The Tower descends above to denote Absalom's house.

Two GUARDS *appear before it carrying their staves.* ABSALOM *enters on the inner stage, hand in hand with* TAMAR, *still veiled, and two more* GUARDS *behind them.*

YONADAB: (*To* GUARDS *out front*) I have to see the Prince. I bear a message.

ABSALOM: Let him in.

(*He is admitted. The* GUARDS *follow him in. Nervously he bows to* ABSALOM.)

(*Cold*) Well?

YONADAB: Your brother begs you impose what humiliation you choose, only spare his life.

ABSALOM: This is *your* counsel.

YONADAB: No, I am merely his messenger.

ABSALOM: (*To* TAMAR) What do you say to this?

TAMAR: You must decide.

ABSALOM: Then never. Never in this life. Tell him so – your good friend.

YONADAB: No friend of mine.

ABSALOM: Really?

YONADAB: Not any more. He disgusts me.

ABSALOM: Disgusts?

TAMAR: Can Yonadab be disgusted?

ABSALOM: Don't speak with him, Tamar. The companion of beasts is a beast himself.

YONADAB: Not true! I'm not him! I am myself.

TAMAR: And who is that?

(*He kneels to her. She approaches him.*)

ABSALOM: Tamar – I told you. Please go in.

TAMAR: (*Coolly*) Pardon me, brother.

(*She stops before* YONADAB *and unveils.*)

YONADAB: (*To audience, on his knees*) Astounding. She had changed completely. In one short week – as if lodging with him had done it. Prettiness had left her – that petty prettiness of youth – and in its place a beauty had suddenly come: as clear as his. Where there'd always been a pouting mask was now a face. She had become a Shiner too. (*To her*) Princess . . . You are superb.

(*She stares at him.*)

ABSALOM: (*To his* GUARDS, *sharply*) Take her in.

TAMAR: I do not need to be taken, thank you.

(*On an impulse* YONADAB *kisses her hand. She withdraws it, veils herself and departs. He watches her leave, fascinated. Possessed with rage,* ABSALOM *moves forward and smacks him in the face.*)

ABSALOM: You will never speak to her again – am I heard? (*He grabs him by the hair.*) I did not swear to spare you, Yonadab! I could slit you like a sheep and no oath broken! Take care . . . Take much care. I have not done with you. I warned you – *I will know everything!*

YONADAB: *Stop it!*

ABSALOM: I'm not a fool – *Yonadab.* I'm not my brother. I could cut you now and watch with joy! Joy! Joy! *Joy!* – do you understand?

YONADAB: (*Breaking free and suddenly raging back*) All right! *Do it! Go on then! Slit! Slash! Slit!* DO IT! (*Pause.*) Whatever made me think you could be different? 'Joy! Joy!' You're all the same – David's savages!

(*He stands glaring at* ABSALOM, *who stands glaring back and hissing.*)

(*To audience*) Whatever gave me the guts to speak like *that*? Indifference, my dears. What I'd told his drunken brother was the literal truth. I truly didn't care any more.

(*To* ABSALOM) Go on. Go on – *cut me!* It's all you know or ever will! And he thinks you're Chosen! (*He laughs shrilly.*) *You – Prince of Peace!!*

(*Pause.*)

ABSALOM: What are you saying?

YONADAB: (*Bitterly*) Nothing! What does it matter? It's all just an endless joke!

ABSALOM: (*Insistent*) What do you mean – 'Chosen'?

YONADAB: He thinks bedding his sister can turn a Prince into a God.

ABSALOM: I know that! I've heard it all from the Princess – blasphemous filth!

YONADAB: Yes, well now he thinks it's *you*.

ABSALOM: What?

YONADAB: Not him – *you* who has been ordained, all the time! Quite a surprise, isn't it? He told me all the Signs for it this afternoon.

ABSALOM: (*Contemptuously*) What Signs?

YONADAB: Does it matter? The man is obviously deranged.

ABSALOM: All the same I'll know what he says about me.

YONADAB: The purest nonsense. I'll go home now, if you please.

ABSALOM: (*Seizing him with sudden speed*) You will stay here until I give you *leave* to go.

(*The* GUARDS *raise their staves.*)

YONADAB: (*Looking straight at him*) I am your cousin, Absalom, not your cur. Treat me so or stay in ignorance.

(*Pause.* ABSALOM *furiously digests this. Then he lets* YONADAB *go.*)

And alone, please.

(ABSALOM *claps violently, dismissing his* GUARDS, *who leave very reluctantly. He now has difficulty in concealing his interest.*)

ABSALOM: So then? These Signs. What are they, these great Signs I am – what's the word? Ordained?

YONADAB: They're not exactly profound.

ABSALOM: I hardly expect them to be. Well?

YONADAB: (*Drily*) They are three in number. First, your hair.

ABSALOM: What?

YONADAB: Your lordship's famous hair. That is apparently very significant.

ABSALOM: Are you making game of me?

YONADAB: Not at all. Apparently it's well known that men chosen for special Destiny have special features.

(*Lights up more on* AMNON *on the outer stage. He speaks, adopting the same 'prophetic' posture he used in the preceding scene with* YONADAB. *There is now a Three-cornered Scene:* AMNON *in the past addressing* YONADAB; YONADAB *continuing in the present.*)

AMNON: (*Drunk and fervent*) Think of it! Not even Samson had hair like that – and he was a Chosen Man. How much more must this one be! And that is only the First Sign.

ABSALOM: (*Sarcastic*) Wonderful. What's the Second?

AMNON: (*Impressively*) *How did she find him?* The whole city speaks of it. She walked straight to his house through that maze of streets, looking neither to right nor left. A girl who had never been there in her life!

ABSALOM: Well, she asked the way!

YONADAB: (*Still dry*) They say not.

AMNON: An invisible hand led her, Yonadab!

ABSALOM: (*Mocking*) Oh yes, of course! Naturally!

AMNON: Try and understand! It was all *ordained* – every moment of it – right from the start! I had to cast her out so he could take her in. Now I must be destroyed so they can be created. It's all foreseen! The two Beauties of the Tribe together! And *full*, you see – full brother and sister, not just half, like me. It's all so clear. The ancient legend is being fulfilled again. A Kingdom of Peace ruled over by two lovers – closest in blood – and immortal! A young God and Goddess!

ABSALOM: Astounding! A Prince of Israel talking like this! Astounding!

YONADAB: When men are determined to believe nonsense, there's no preventing them.

ABSALOM: Go on.

YONADAB: I'd rather not.

ABSALOM: Why?

YONADAB: You won't care for it.

ABSALOM: No matter: finish. What is the Third Wondrous Sign?

AMNON: Most convincing of all! A man has to be *pure* to be chosen. That's obvious. How could it ever have been *me*, with all my women? He's different! Who has ever seen Absalom with a woman? Final and clearest Sign! A man of twenty-two years: most loved in all the land: most virtuous: most beautiful: and still virgin.

ABSALOM: What??!

YONADAB: You made me tell you. Remember that!

(ABSALOM *bursts into outraged laughter.*)

ABSALOM: Poor fool! *Poor stupid idiot!* For what it's worth that last Sign isn't even true. He's not only stupid – but wrong as well!

YONADAB: Well, of course, I told him that.

ABSALOM: Completely and entirely wrong! . . . *Wrong!*

YONADAB: 'A man of Prince Absalom's maturity,' I said – 'do you imagine he could still possibly be in that condition? With every woman in Israel besotted with him?'

ABSALOM: What did he say to that?

YONADAB: He wouldn't listen.

AMNON: (*Smugly impervious*) It's all foreseen! It's all foreseen, Yonadab!

YONADAB: As I said – when men are determined to believe nonsense, there's no preventing them.

(*Pause.*)

ABSALOM: (*Brusquely*) Leave me now. Don't return.

YONADAB: You mean never?

ABSALOM: Yes.

YONADAB: I would much like to.

ABSALOM: Why?

YONADAB: I would be your man, if you would let me.

ABSALOM: You would be anybody's man, I think.
YONADAB: You don't know me.
ABSALOM: I do not wish to. Go now.

(*He makes a gesture of dismissal.* YONADAB *bows.*)

YONADAB: May your days always fatten.

(*He bows and departs.* ABSALOM *stays for a moment looking after him, unconsciously fingering his own hair.*)

(*To audience*) How strange it was. I, who had entered his house so frightened, now hated to leave. He seemed to me as his father must have once seemed – the boldest spirit shining through the flesh. I stood there in my own new boldness spying on him – and as I did, something astounding happened. Another curtain fell!

(*Music.* ABSALOM *unlooses his hair. It falls in an amazing cascade to well below his shoulders.*)

But this time not hiding anything. Showing!

(ABSALOM *turns, running his hands through it.*)

I had never seen it loose before. If I'd been anyone but Yonadab the Cynic, I might indeed have taken it for a Sign myself! To this hour, talking to you in Eternity, I recall the sight. It has made a perpetual ghost in my ghost's head. Absalom turning in his miraculous mantle. And she with him – his ravishing sister. Two beings I had so long disliked – holding me there by the rope of pure beauty.

(TAMAR *appears. She curtsies to her brother. He reaches out to her – but she eludes him with a smile and goes out again. He follows her eagerly. The music stops. The Tower retires, above the inner stage.* YONADAB *reluctantly leaves it and walks down to where* AMNON *sits brooding.*)

AMNON: What did he say?
YONADAB: He will not forgive you.
AMNON: (*Rising portentously*) He can't. The Gods forbid him to. I must die so he can live for ever.
YONADAB: (*Impatiently*) Oh, Amnon – please!
AMNON: It is ordained!

(*He goes off unsteadily.*)

SCENE FIVE

The lights go down more.

YONADAB: (*To audience*) And now the stillest time set in. Everyone stayed in his own corner. Amnon babbling nonsense in his house. Absalom and Tamar locked away in theirs.
(DAVID *appears on the inner stage.*)
And King David wandering the rooms of his palace, beseeching Heaven. I caught him at it one afternoon – up to my favourite game of watching unseen. And again I was rewarded for it with one of the rarest sights in the world. And do you know the most surprising thing about it? I'd always imagined when he addressed his God it was with enormous reverence: Thees and Thous and deep Conjuration. Not a bit. He spoke to him exactly like an honest workman to an impossible employer.

DAVID: A Sign! That's all I'm asking. One Sign! Is that too much? Yes – I wronged her. I admit it. She got no comfort from me. But did she come for it? You saw! She went straight to *him*. Deliberately! Proudly – straight *to him*, in front of the whole city. Was this well done? . . . Or was this *you*? Did you put it in her mind? 'Go to Absalom – David is finished!'? Am I dismissed – is that it? Or is this still my punishment for Bathsheba? *Surely not*. When you took my first son with her, I thought we were quits for that. Am I wrong? Am I mistaken again? Is it to go on for all my life? Great God, did you even *cause* all this? – plant the lust in Amnon for his sister *yourself*? Would you do that? You couldn't! You wouldn't *surely*? (*He covers his mouth.*) Forgive my most sinful mouth. Your ways are not ours and none shall know them. (*Desperately*) O Lord, a *Sign*! Just one! Tell me your will: it's all I ask. Is it to be Mercy or Justice? If Mercy for the boy, the girl is cheated. If Justice, then I must kill the boy. And I *will* – you know that. I'll smash the first stone on him myself. I'll see his blood on my palm – not wash it for a month. I'll wear it as the most precious ointment! (*Humbly*) But if I am still even a little acceptable in your sight – I beg you: let it be Mercy.

Forget Justice for this once. Don't force me to bitterness for the rest of life. Leave me my Bull . . .
(*Pause.*)
(*Yearningly*) And, whatever thy will, speak to me again as you did when I still pleased you.
(DAVID *leaves the stage.*)

SCENE SIX

YONADAB: (*To audience*) I scuttled home quickly and locked the doors. Perhaps it wasn't over yet with my great Challenge. A voice could still whisper out of the vast dark to his royal ears – '*Yonadab. Yonadab did it. Kill Yonadab for Justice!*'
(*A strange music starts. He lies down on the outer stage.*)
And now for three nights in succession the same amazing dream appeared to me. So clear I could almost touch the figures in it.
(*The music rises. On the inner stage we see, glittering in slow motion, what he describes. The* HELPERS *bear brother and sister as if on horses, both their arms outstretched, their faces smiling.*)
Absalom and Tamar, riding together upon huge golden horses – jouncing and gleeful up the high road to Jerusalem! On their heads sat golden crowns. On their shoulders golden cloaks. And from their palms streamed golden light. I knelt in the dust and reached up to them to greet them. They bowed to me – and I saw that their tongues were of gold also – like the clappers of bells, tolling out one word. One word rolling over the desert!

TWO VOICES: (*Male and female, as before, filling the theatre*) PEACE! PEACE! . . . *PEACE*!
(*A bang on the floor from the stave held by one of Absalom's* GUARDS *cuts off the sound. The light changes. The riders disappear.* YONADAB *scrambles hastily to his feet.*)

YONADAB: What do you want?

(*The* GUARD *motions with his staff towards the inner stage, where the Tower is now descending.*)

Absalom? He has sent for me?

(*The* GUARD *nods. Two* HELPERS *bring in torches on to the inner stage.*)

Summoned! What could it mean? Summoned – in the middle of the night!

(*He goes with the* GUARD *upstage.* ABSALOM *appears on the inner stage, grim-faced and disturbed.*)

SCENE SEVEN

YONADAB: My Prince! How may I help you?

ABSALOM: (*Curtly*) Blasphemy: that's the way!

YONADAB: (*Alarmed*) What do you mean?

ABSALOM: The King cannot refuse to judge him for blasphemy. You can be the witness – then he'll *have* to act.

YONADAB: No!

ABSALOM: You said you wish to be my man.

YONADAB: I did.

ABSALOM: So be.

YONADAB: Not with this. Amnon was my friend, whatever he is now.

ABSALOM: He is a blasphemer now. The most flagrant.

YONADAB: And so he must die?

ABSALOM: The Law is clear. 'Cursed be he who lieth with his sister. He shall be cut off in the sight of the People.'

YONADAB: 'And all the People shall say Amen.'

ABSALOM: Yes.

YONADAB: Of course. What else do they ever say? A death and another death and another! Saul hath slain his thousands and David his tens of thousands. And how many will you slay when it's your turn?

ABSALOM: I don't seek this for myself. It is the Law.

YONADAB: (*Firmly*) I will not deliver him to death, Absalom, and that is that.

ABSALOM: The man has sought to make himself a God. *The heir to our throne!*

YONADAB: Not any more.

ABSALOM: What do you mean?

YONADAB: You know what I mean.

ABSALOM: Who else? Who else is heir?

YONADAB: Oh, Prince, please – let's not play. You know who will inherit now as well as I.

ABSALOM: Be silent! Great Father alone will decide that.

YONADAB: The People will decide it – and you know how.

ABSALOM: Tssss! I could have you judged for that!

YONADAB: (*Impertinently*) And cut off – cut off in the sight of the People. Amen for ever! Amen, amen, amen, amen!

(*Pause.* ABSALOM *glares at him.*)

Forgive me. I'm not myself tonight. I think I should go home.

ABSALOM: Yes! Quick! Before I call the men. Go! *Get out!*

(YONADAB *bows and starts to go.*)

Stay.

(*A long pause.*)

(*Shyly*) Do you truly think what you said? That I could reign next?

YONADAB: There's no 'could' about it. Even my dreams announce it – for what that's worth.

ABSALOM: Your dreams?

YONADAB: Three nights on end I have actually seen you crowned.

ABSALOM: Crowned? How?

YONADAB: It's not worth saying. Dreams are all nonsense.

ABSALOM: All the same – oblige me. Tell.

YONADAB: I have to warn you, I dream as often as pigs grunt. And with as much consequence for the world.

ABSALOM: (*Stiffly*) Still – please. I beg you.

(*Pause.*)

Absalom begs. Tell me.

YONADAB: Then Yonadab obeys. (*To audience as* ABSALOM

freezes) Of course I had to. The Shiner begging! That was like the School Hero begging from the grubby New Boy. I was flattered to death. I told my dream to him, my dears, with as much dash as I could. And he listened like one possessed.

ABSALOM: Light! From our palms?

YONADAB: Yes – streaming.

ABSALOM: And 'Peace'. The word we call out is 'Peace'?

YONADAB: No mistaking that. It's not a word one hears too often.

ABSALOM: How wonderful if it were ever honoured in this land above 'War'.

YONADAB: (*Surprised*) You think so?

ABSALOM: (*Simply*) Truly. Yes.

YONADAB: Your father is a man of war.

ABSALOM: He is the greatest warrior in the world. How fine if I could excel him in one thing. A man of Peace! *Three times* you've dreamt this? That could mean something.

YONADAB: To those who believe in dreams, three is a highly significant number, I understand. (*Sheepishly*) Also I have to admit I did actually dream of you once before – and it came true, quite literally. It was a situation totally unconnected with Peace. In fact I bear the scars from it still.

ABSALOM: When I threw you out of doors?

YONADAB: I dreamed that scene exactly, in every detail, before it happened.

ABSALOM: No!

YONADAB: As I live. However, I'm aware it would actually be impossible for any sane man to mistake me for a prophet.

ABSALOM: You're a very strange fellow, Yonadab. I have no idea who you are.

YONADAB: Nor I you.

(TAMAR *enters.* ABSALOM *is now evidently deeply excited and disturbed by what he has heard.*)

TAMAR: I have prepared the food as you asked me. With my own hands. It's laid ready in the Tower.

ABSALOM: Good . . . Yes . . . Very good. (*To* YONADAB) Come back tomorrow.

YONADAB: If you wish.

ABSALOM: This same time. Don't fail.

YONADAB: I promise. (*To* TAMAR) Princess – excuse me.

TAMAR: (*Gently*) Yonadab.

(*She smiles at him for the first time. He bows to her.* ABSALOM *claps sharply.*)

ABSALOM: (*To* YONADAB) Go now. We would be alone.

YONADAB: I'm sorry. Forgive me . . . I'm off . . . Of course!

(*He retires hastily on to the outer stage.*)

(*To audience*) But of course I couldn't leave. Not now. Something wild was obviously working in him. And she – smiling at me like that! What could it mean? The Spy inside me was shrieking like mad: 'Get up there into that tower – quickly! Something big is about to happen!' I needed no second bidding. In moments like this Advanced Voyeurs have unerring instinct! Quick as thought I ran up the stairs ahead of them – twice as fast as I'd run back into Amnon's house that terrible night.

(*He runs back on to the inner stage. Music starts low. Two* HELPERS *bring in a rack of gorgeous cloaks – amongst them the one which* ABSALOM *wrapped around* TAMAR *at the end of Act One. Another* HELPER *brings in a plate of cakes.*)

The room was very small. In the corner was an alcove, filled with his cloaks: just room enough to hide! I rushed into it – engulfed at once in his sweet smell: so different from the rancid stench of Amnon. My heart was pounding so hard they must surely hear it!

SCENE EIGHT

ABSALOM *and* TAMAR *move slowly to the cakes and sit.*

YONADAB: (*To audience*) What follows now is the truest story: I swear it. Not the events recorded in your Bible – but the reason *for* the events. Seen by no man but me. Spoken by no man ever – till now. To you. By one who wishes he had never gone into that Tower. Fool. Fool. Fool that I was! If only I'd guessed! If only I'd seen what she was up to! What she *had* to be up to! Alas: the instinct I talk about was all for spying. In matters that counted I was blind as a baby! If I had been half as clever as I thought I was, I would have seen it plain. But then who is? Can *you* guess – any of *you*?

(ABSALOM *sits.* YONADAB *watches avidly from among the cloaks.*)

ABSALOM: Tamar's cakes.

TAMAR: If your men knew, they would throw them from the window. Where they want to throw *me*.

ABSALOM: You?

TAMAR: Oh, yes. They say I'm a witch.

ABSALOM: No!

TAMAR: I hear them talking among themselves. 'Poor Amnon,' they say. 'That girl made him cakes and put a spell on them. What chance did he have after that?'

ABSALOM: They are ignorant men. They don't even know witches are ugly.

TAMAR: You should beware. Don't eat or you may feel the way your brother did.

ABSALOM: Give me one.

TAMAR: (*Proffering the plate*) Here.

ABSALOM: On your hand.

(*She puts a cake on her hand, and extends it.*)

TAMAR: Say the Blessing first.

ABSALOM: No!

TAMAR: Say it.

ABSALOM: Blessed are thou, O King of the Universe – who has given us food from lovely women.

TAMAR: Tss! Don't blaspheme.

ABSALOM: Forgive me!

(*He lowers his head and eats from her hand.*)

TAMAR: You are disturbed.

ABSALOM: Am I?

TAMAR: I heard you walking in here last night for hours. Is it to do with Yonadab?

ABSALOM: Perhaps. You smiled at him downstairs.

TAMAR: Did I?

ABSALOM: Why?

TAMAR: Why not?

ABSALOM: Amnon's friend. You smile at Amnon's friend?

TAMAR: He is no longer that. He told us so.

ABSALOM: You unveiled yourself to him when you saw him last. Why did you do that?

TAMAR: And you struck him after I left: why did *you* do *that*? You didn't think I saw, but I did.

ABSALOM: I thought you hated him.

TAMAR: He was hateful then.

ABSALOM: But not any more?

TAMAR: I don't know him any more. He disturbs me also.

ABSALOM: What do you mean?

TAMAR: I see him sometimes in my dreams. Isn't that weird? Quite often, actually. Always the same dream.

ABSALOM: What?

TAMAR: Really quite wonderful. I love it when it comes . . .

ABSALOM: (*Alarmed*) Why? What happens in it? Say!

TAMAR: It's quite marvellous. Everything is gold. We're on huge horses – you and I – and they're all gold. We're wearing gold crowns on our heads. And this is the best thing, our tongues are gold too. They look like those things inside bells. And they only say one word. Over and over again.

ABSALOM: (*Whispering*) 'Peace.'

TAMAR: (*Startled*) How do you know?

ABSALOM: Go on.

TAMAR: How do you know that? You can't possibly know that!

ABSALOM: Please, Tamar. What about Yonadab?

TAMAR: He's kneeling on the ground by the city gate. He's reaching up to us with such a look of joy on his face. Not creepy at all, like he is in life.

ABSALOM: And we bow to him.

TAMAR: Yes! *How do you know? How do you know any of this?*

ABSALOM: *Because he dreams it too!*

TAMAR: No!

ABSALOM: Every detail is the same! He's dreamt it too three nights on end. I swear it. You can ask him tomorrow.

(*A pause. They stare at each other in astonishment.* YONADAB, *who has heard all this, stands equally amazed.*)

TAMAR: What does it mean?

ABSALOM: Answer one question.

TAMAR: What?

ABSALOM: When you came to this house that morning – did you know the way?

(*She gives a little gasp.*)

Or did someone point it out?

(*She looks away.*)

Please, Tamar. I need to know. (*Pause.*) Which? Why don't you answer? Tamar!

TAMAR: (*Awkwardly*) I never mentioned it before – because I thought you would laugh.

ABSALOM: Yes?

TAMAR: That morning – I didn't know where your house was in the whole city. How could I? I'd never been in the streets before. I only knew I had to find you. I knew that absolutely. I had to find this house and not ask the way from anyone. Don't ask me why. And I did. I just walked. As if I was being led. It was weird. As if there was actually a hand in mine, pulling me on – only gently. On and on. That's how it felt. As if my feet weren't my own. Why are you asking this now?

(*But* ABSALOM *has covered his mouth in wonder.* YONADAB, *as before, is equally astounded.*)

Absalom? What is it? . . . Is it a bad omen?

ABSALOM: I . . . have to tell you something also now.

TAMAR: (*Very anxious*) What have I said? Tell me! Please!

ABSALOM: (*Rising*) Swear to be secret.

TAMAR: Of course.

ABSALOM: No, no – swear it. What I tell you now is for you alone. Swear.

(*Bewilderedly the girl gives the sign for oath on her head.* ABSALOM *walks about the room, very upset. He speaks with difficulty.*)

Before you came here – that dreadful day – I . . . I had never in my life sought women. I am, as it's said . . . virgin . . . After – when you were torn, it was like something in me was torn as well. A seal, broken . . . As if I'd been waiting here all the time for it. For you.

(A pause. He looks at her, trembling.)

I believe something has happened. Something greater than anything we've known. You were *sent* to me – not able to help yourself. And I was waiting here – not able to help myself either.

TAMAR: I don't understand.

ABSALOM: Don't be frightened. (*Very seriously*) I think we have been Chosen, Tamar. You and I.

TAMAR: Chosen? What for?

ABSALOM: I have a dream too. Only one, and it's horrible. I'm in his bedroom – Amnon's – and I see you there on his bed. I can't move to help you. I just have to watch. I see him pushing you, and shouting 'Get out!' I'm shouting too! 'Come to me! Come to me! I'll take you in. I'll take you in for ever!' But you can't hear me! . . . I wake up shouting it.

TAMAR: I've heard you in the night. I didn't know what it meant . . .

(*A pause.*)

(*Not moving*) Say them again, those words, now you're awake.

ABSALOM: (*Shyly*) Come to me: I'll take you in for ever.

TAMAR: To *me.*

ABSALOM: (*To her*) Come to me. I'll take you in for ever.

(*She goes to him.*)

TAMAR: I have come.

ABSALOM: I love you, Tamar. It's true . . .

(*A pause.*)

TAMAR: I love you also, my dear. I've hidden it so much. I've tried to hide it and hide it . . . I *love you, Absalom!*

ABSALOM: Oh, Tamar!

TAMAR: It's *meant* – I know it too! It's *meant for us*!

ABSALOM: To love?

TAMAR: And rule! Rule together! I believe it!

ABSALOM: And something more! Perhaps something even more! Even more!

TAMAR: What?

ABSALOM: I daren't speak it! I can't believe it myself . . .

TAMAR: What?

ABSALOM: Oh, Tamar! Oh, dear girl – *let it be!*

(*He kisses her passionately. She surrenders to him. Music rises.* YONADAB *steps forward, deeply moved, Absalom's cloak in his hand.*)

YONADAB: (*To audience*) In a trance I watched it happen. Those two enfold – mingling their beauties together. And for the first time in my life I knew the force of prayer. Yes! As they stood there, unmoving, I called to them without any sound his words, 'Let it be! Let it be!' . . . These Signs are overwhelming even to me! Confound me utterly, Yonadab the Sneerer! *Let it be!* I know Gods cannot walk on earth: *let it be*! I know lovers cannot infect Kingdoms: *let it be*! Let there be an end to this world of blood-soaked worship – and to my own world too, which owns no worship! *Make me see it!* Change my unchanging world! Set this manipulating man at last in ways of *Meaning*! *Why else was I born with such urgency of spirit, and nothing for urgency to move?* (*Directly*) Imagine this, if you can. I, the smart son of countless sightless nomads, starved for pictures in pictureless Jerusalem, imploring a boy and girl as if to effigies or holy statues long denied – 'Let it be! Let it be! Let me believe!' And in the drench of it I bowed my head into the cloak with which he had wrapped her, as into the veil of a Temple. I wiped my dissolving eyes as on the fringes of the holiest prayer shawl.

(*He sighs aloud. They turn and see him.*)

(*To them*) Forgive me! I have heard everything.

ABSALOM: (*Entranced*) Is it possible? We are like those lovers in the Legend? Can this be possible?

YONADAB: Certainly some great mystery is working through you both. (*Impulsively*) Yes! I believe you have been chosen as surely as Samuel chose your father!

ABSALOM: Then you are *our* Samuel.

YONADAB: No.

ABSALOM: This must be your destiny: to tell us.

YONADAB: No.

ABSALOM: Of course! You came to me just as surely as she did – not knowing *yourself*! You dreamed her dream, and brought it to me. You told me all the Signs – too many to be ignored.

YONADAB: Yes, but not me! It can't possibly be me.

ABSALOM: Why not?

YONADAB: (*Crying out*) Because I'm Yonadab! *I'm Nobody!* (*Pause.*)

ABSALOM: If we are Chosen – then so are you. We bow to you. (ABSALOM *and* TAMAR *bow to* YONADAB. *He goes to them in wonder and takes their hands. He kneels to them, placing his brow on their joined hands.*)
(*Gently*) We are Chosen, my friend. I believe you absolutely. We must take this Kingdom now and bring it Peace. The Kingdom of Peace! I feel it growing inside me – the gift of rule. My heart is bursting, Yonadab. I want to cry it out from here to all the city!

YONADAB: (*Alarmed*) I beg you not to!

ABSALOM: Why?

YONADAB: The People are not remotely prepared for this. Even adored as you are, they wouldn't take it.

TAMAR: He's right.

ABSALOM: So what do I do? You must advise me.

TAMAR: Advise us both, Yonadab.

YONADAB: Of course you must speak to the Tribe – but not yet. The time isn't ripe yet.

TAMAR: When *will* it be?

ABSALOM: When Father's dead. That's what he means. Father must die first – isn't that it?

TAMAR: You mean we must kill him?

ABSALOM: Of course not. His days are numbered – that's what he means. We simply ride into the city like in the dream – and David will *topple*! The Gods will strike him dead. Isn't that right? They will make the way clear for us?

YONADAB: (*Nervously*) I'm not sure. I don't think it works exactly like that.

ABSALOM: He'll not be able to stand against us, if it's *meant*! That's obvious! (*To* TAMAR) But first we do what we're ordained to do. First – we must complete our love!

TAMAR: No, not first.

ABSALOM: What do you mean?

TAMAR: First comes Justice: then love.

(*Pause.*)
First Amnon must die. At your hands.

ABSALOM: Tamar!

TAMAR: Only a just man can take Father's place. The People must see that clearly.

ABSALOM: They see it now. It's why they love me!

TAMAR: They see only weakness now. Even your own men. I hear them every day behind your back. 'When do we do it? When is he going to act like a man?'

ABSALOM: That's not true!

TAMAR: Of course it is. They will never accept you till you do it – say what you like.

ABSALOM: I gave an oath. Have you forgotten that?

TAMAR: (*Sharply*) Yes – which shames you.

ABSALOM: What?

TAMAR: Shames – yes! As Father intended.

ABSALOM: Tamar!

TAMAR: You know how he works. This way you can never move against him. His dupe, that's all you are.

ABSALOM: Be silent.

TAMAR: Dupe.

ABSALOM: Tssss.

TAMAR: His fool!

ABSALOM: Tssss!

TAMAR: Tell him, Yonadab! Speak.

YONADAB: (*Cautiously*) It is certainly true – any man who would replace David must first break David's chain.

TAMAR: There!

ABSALOM: I gave an oath, and will not break it. There – from me!

TAMAR: Good: then I won't break mine. See now: I swear! (*She puts her hand on her head.*) Until Amnon is dead, Absalom will never lie with me in love. Selah! (*Appealing*) One death – that's all I'm asking.

ABSALOM: I gave my oath, Tamar. A King with no oath is nothing.

TAMAR: A real King does not need it. People follow him wherever he leads. Strength – strength is what they want! Tell him, Yonadab.

(*Both look to* YONADAB, *who stands in discomfort.*)

ABSALOM: (*To* YONADAB) What do I do? You tell me! . . . Kill your friend – is that what you want? Answer!

TAMAR: Unless you do – all will stay as it is. (*Grandly*) I have sworn now.

(ABSALOM *stands like an animal at bay, baffled and raging.*)

ABSALOM: Peace? . . . Haaa! *Peace?!* . . .

(*He gives a sudden impotent snarl of fury and rushes away offstage. A pause.* TAMAR *is alone with* YONADAB.)

TAMAR: You must persuade him.

YONADAB: (*Startled*) I?

TAMAR: He believes in you. As I do. We have shared the same dream. That binds us.

YONADAB: A dream without blood, Princess.

TAMAR: As long as Amnon lives that is impossible. He will rule next and we will be destroyed – Chosen or not. You as well.

YONADAB: No . . .

TAMAR: He'll never trust you again, knowing you knelt to his brother. He will kill us all: what else can he do?

YONADAB: (*Carefully*) That's true.

(*Pause.*)

TAMAR: One death, and all that would change. Love would reign here . . . And you would be our Chief Counsellor.

(*Pause. Her voice becomes more winning.*)

Can't you make him see this? In his heart he wants it deeply. Be his Samuel, as he calls you, and speak to him . . . Please . . .

YONADAB: How you have changed.

TAMAR: I?

YONADAB: In a few bare weeks. I see it so clearly.

TAMAR: I'll swear something else to you. If you persuade him – you will be my brother also.

(*She lightly touches her head again then transfers her fingers to his mouth.*)

Truly.

YONADAB: (*To audience*) Lost! At that moment I was lost beyond recall. Within one single day, my dears, I became a Prophet: a Mini-Samuel. Yonadab the Soothsayer. It's actually a fairly easy role to play if you have been starved for attention all your life. All it takes is a taste for theatrics and the right tremble in the vocal cords.

SCENE NINE

ABSALOM *marches in from upstage with four armed* GUARDS.

YONADAB: (*Impressively to* ABSALOM, *hands raised aloft*) I say to you Everything on earth begins in blood. All of Mankind and all that it fashions. Even Peace itself! Amnon is the violence you rebuke. Let the world see you do it. Let *me* see it – even I, who was his friend. Man thirsts for Righteousness. Blessed be he who slakes that thirst!
(*The* GUARDS *bang their staves appreciatively*.)
Just one act of blood and no more. One blow for the Kingdom of Peace. Raise the sword once – then lay it down for ever.
(TAMAR *claps: all freeze*.)
(*To audience*) Wasn't that splendid? Just one more blow, and everything will be all right ever more! One more bullet – one more bomb – one more Exocet and exorcism is done!

TAMAR: Listen to him, Absalom. He knows.

ABSALOM: I hear.

TAMAR: It's sense!

ABSALOM: It still cannot be done! Father has placed thirty guards around him. Do you want a slaughter? And here, in the Holy City?

YONADAB: So do it *out* of the city.

ABSALOM: How? He never leaves his house.

YONADAB: Go to the King and implore his pardon. As proof you mean it, invite him to your estate at Ba'al Hazoor. Next month is the sheep-shearing. Offer him a feast.

ABSALOM: (*Testily*) What's the good of that? He'll only refuse – the same as always.

YONADAB: Then beg for your brothers to go in his stead. *All* of them. Amnon too. Say you long to be reconciled with him.

ABSALOM: He won't believe it.

YONADAB: He's desperate for an end to this. He'll thank you.

ABSALOM: Never.

YONADAB: Believe me. I *know* . . .

ABSALOM: But the lies! The deceit of it – to his face . . .

YONADAB: Your father has often said Deceit is justified in the cause of Right.

TAMAR: That's true. I've heard him.

YONADAB: And only his God knows what things he's done himself with that excuse. It will work, Absalom. It's all he longs for, night and day: for his Bull to be forgiven. Trust me.

(*Longer pause.*)

ABSALOM: (*Decisively, to his* GUARDS) Come. We go to court.

(*The staves bang enthusiastically.*)

TAMAR: No! Only you. Not these. Show them who you mean to be. A man unarmed except in Justice.

YONADAB: She's right. A band of men will scare him.

TAMAR: (*Going to him; affectionately*) Go alone. Get the permission, that's all. Yonadab will do the rest with Amnon. And afterwards, I will do more with you.

(*She kisses him on the lips. The* GUARDS *watch, startled.*)

YONADAB: (*Sotto voce*) Caution, I beg you.

(*Brother and sister move apart.*)

TAMAR: May I beg one favour from you now?

ABSALOM: Anything!

TAMAR: After this is done, disown these men. That will prove to everyone you mean Peace.

(*The men look at their master anxiously.*)

ABSALOM: (*To* YONADAB) What do you say to that?

YONADAB: Certainly it would be the clearest gesture.

TAMAR: Let me have them instead – for my protection.

(*The men stir, alarmed.*)

Giving them up would speak louder than any words.

ABSALOM: She's right of course. (*To her*) Your pain has made you wise beyond your little years.

YONADAB: It's true, Prince.

ABSALOM: (*Fondly*) You will teach us all. And we will learn – I promise you! (*To his* GUARDS) Hear me. From the moment Prince Amnon dies you will serve the Princess Tamar only – to be her men. For her safekeeping.

(*They growl and stir in protest.*)

Be silent! I give you the blood you want – that's enough! Am I heard?

(*They bang their staves with fury.*)

What is this? Do you defy me?

(*Again they bang.*)

Tssss! You are bonded to my bidding – have you forgotten? Now *do it*. Swear to me all of you, on your heads. 'From Amnon's death you will be Tamar's men. Never to be discharged except by her.'

(*They hesitate.*)

Swear.

(*They clap their hands to their heads in the ritual gesture.*)

Good. Now he's cursed who ever breaks this oath.

(TAMAR *takes* ABSALOM*'s hands.*)

So I give up wrath. I am not David but David's son. Gentleness will have its birth in Israel. And all shall see it.

YONADAB: A new kind of King.

TAMAR: King – yes!

ABSALOM: (*To his* GUARDS) Take her in. Care only for her. That is my command to you from this day on.

(*He claps his hands. Reluctantly the* GUARDS *move and escort* TAMAR *offstage. The light changes. The Tower withdraws out of sight.* YONADAB *moves to the side of the stage.* ABSALOM *stands alone in the middle.*)

SCENE TEN

The palace.

Music sounds. With an elaborate gesture, ABSALOM *throws himself headlong on to his face and lies prone.*

YONADAB: (*To audience*) And then – for half a day – Absalom lay at the door of his father's chamber. Tears bathed his face – and the faces of those who saw him.

(DAVID *appears. He extends his hand.*)

And the King was moved to great joy.

DAVID: The Sign! His Sign! A young man thrown down by love. Filled till he overflows, with penitence! How dare I stand before him and not forgive? I thank Thee, O God, for showing me my way! (*To* ABSALOM) Do you beg mercy for him, your shameful brother?

ABSALOM: I do, Beloved Father.

DAVID: Then shall it be! Not mere Justice that hurts as it's delivered – but Mercy that *heals*! Rise now. Come to me. (*Calling out*) Boys!

(*He raises and embraces* ABSALOM *fervently.*)

Oh, Absalom, my darling child! My own!

(*Four* HELPERS *come on as* ADONIJAH, ITHREAM, SHOBAB *and* SHEPATIAH.)

(*To them, beside himself*) Tell your brothers Amnon is forgiven! His crime is wiped away with love! You will go into the country for a Feast – and Amnon will go with you! Treat him well. Tell him God has pardoned him through the mouth of his brother, the loving . . . You were always the sweetest. How else could it ever have come, mercy, except through you? Take them, my Shiner! Feast them till they burst! And when you have done, bring him back to me – that Bull of mine – and I will forgive him also! Oh! Oh! . . . Go with him now, all of you – you have my blessing! Bless you all! Bless you! And you *above* all – Absalom! My sweet Shiner!

(*He raises his hands and blesses them as they bow to him and depart. He goes off another way, beside himself with joy.*)

SCENE ELEVEN

AMNON *stumbles on to the outer stage.*

YONADAB: (*To* AMNON) You should have seen the happiness in the King's face.

AMNON: (*Stubbornly*) Well, I'm not going.

YONADAB: (*Aghast*) Why not?

AMNON: Because I don't believe it.

YONADAB: But it's true!

AMNON: It smells. I smell it. There's something else.

YONADAB: (*Exasperated*) Then don't go. Stay in this room for the rest of your life.
(*Long pause.*)

AMNON: Does he truly forgive me?

YONADAB: I have told you.

AMNON: Then why didn't he come himself? One Prince to another?

YONADAB: Because I *asked* to come! Is that so wrong? You begged me to help you – I did. Is it such vanity to want to give you the news myself?
(*Pause.* AMNON *embraces him sloppily.*)

AMNON: You're the greatest friend a man ever had. Ever since the Day of Creation!

YONADAB: God did not create friends, as I recall. Male and Female created he them. There's no mention of friends.

AMNON: When I become King I'll remember this. I'll reward you beyond your greatest dreaming . . . even yours! You wait and see. Are you coming too?

YONADAB: No.

AMNON: Why not?

YONADAB: It is entirely an event between Princes – I wouldn't belong.

AMNON: You belong anywhere. Yonny! . . . Yonny Yonadab . . . (*He kisses him again, with relief, and starts to go.*)

YONADAB: One thing.

AMNON: What?

YONADAB: That night – with you and Tamar . . . I watched.

(*Pause.* AMNON *shrugs.*)

AMNON: What's it matter?

YONADAB: I actually saw nothing. You pulled the curtain.

(AMNON *gives an uncertain laugh.*)

Why did you do that?

(*Pause.*)

AMNON: (*Simply*) I wanted to make a Temple . . . A little Temple.

(*He goes offstage, slowly and unsteadily.*)

YONADAB: (*To audience*) What can I say? When I had nothing but desire for faith, I could have betrayed him – with difficulty. Feeling the stir of faith – it was easier. (*Pause.*) So it was that Prince Amnon went to his brother's feast at Ba'al Hazoor.

SCENE TWELVE

Ba'al Hazoor.

A low sustained chord of music. Four HELPERS *enter and spread on the inner stage a huge woollen rug, emblazoned with the Star of David. They bow and conduct* AMNON *on to it. At the same moment* ABSALOM *appears upstage, dressed in a gold cloak. He extends his hands to* AMNON *in peace. They embrace. The* HELPERS *clap their hands.* AMNON *takes the hands of each of the* HELPERS *(now brothers) in turn.* ABSALOM *and* AMNON *both sit. The two other* HELPERS, *also as Princes, enter with a great flagon and a cup. Wine is poured.* AMNON *and* ABSALOM *speak the blessing together.*

AMNON/ABSALOM: (*Together*) Blessed art Thou, King of the Universe, who hast given us the fruit of the vine.

(AMNON *drinks.* ABSALOM *drinks. All the* HELPERS *stamp their feet with pleasure. Wild music breaks out. The* HELPERS *dance, shouting.* ABSALOM *rises and assists* AMNON *to rise. They dance together, as four* HELPERS *retire. At the height of their dancing – a sudden crash in the music. It breaks off.* TAMAR *stands there, also encased in a cloak of bright gold. She is flanked by Absalom's* GUARDS. *They are armed with their staves as usual, but now the tips of them sport sharp metal points. The two* HELPERS, *still playing Princes, rush from the stage in panic. A low drumming begins.* AMNON *looks wildly around him.* TAMAR *points her hand at him in condemnation. The* GUARDS *chase* AMNON *with their spears. He runs from them and, gargling with fear, finally burrows under the rug. Pitilessly the* GUARDS *drive their sharp weapons through it. A great stain of blood appears in the centre of the Star of David.* ABSALOM *and* TAMAR *embrace in triumph. Darkness swallows the inner stage. The rug is removed from it. Great cries fill the theatre: 'Slain! Slain! Slaughtered! Slaughtered!' Light only on* YONADAB *on the outer stage. The cries break off – two* HELPERS *as messengers run in and jog in place down front on the outer stage.)*

YONADAB: (*To audience*) And now a terrible rumour flew up the road from Ba'al Hazoor! News that not only Amnon had been slain, but all the King's sons. *All of them!* Adonijah. Ithream. Chileab. Shobab. Ibhar. Even the youngest, Solomon! It filled Jerusalem with the speed of pestilence! It filled the old man's ears!

SCENE THIRTEEN

Lights up on the inner stage. A cry from the King.

DAVID *stands, frozen open-mouthed in an attitude of agony. The two* MESSENGERS *join the other* HELPERS *who are prostrate around him, as his servants. All start to keen. Their noise is supplemented by a greater noise of mourning in the whole theatre, which rises and rises.* YONADAB *tries to call out to* DAVID: above it from the outer stage.

YONADAB: No! No! It's not true! Not true, my King!

(*But he is unheard.* DAVID *kneels and ritually tears his clothing.* YONADAB, *exasperated, invades the inner stage and grabs* DAVID *by the shoulders, shouting in his face. This sacrilege stops the noise. His* SERVANTS *look up, hissing – their hands over their mouths.*)

(*Trying to keep calm*) It's not true, Lord King. Do not believe it. All your sons are safe. I know this for fact!

DAVID: (*Bewildered*) What?

YONADAB: Your sons are safe. Only one is dead.

DAVID: What do you say? One? Tell me.

(*He crawls up* YONADAB *and hangs around his neck.*)
Tell me . . . Tell me . . . Tell me . . . Tell me! *Tell!*

YONADAB: (*To audience*) Behold the social climax of my life. I stand before the Tribe wearing its King for a pendant.

DAVID: Tell me.

YONADAB: Alone, Lord King.

DAVID: Leave, all – quickly! QUICKLY!

(*All leave.* DAVID *stares at him desperately.*)

YONADAB: Your sons are safe. All except Amnon. On the day he forced your daughter, Absalom swore to kill him. This he has done. But all your other boys you will see again. I swear it. (*Gesture of swearing.*) They will be here with you soon.

(DAVID *moves away from him. A long pause.* DAVID *sits.*)

DAVID: (*Suddenly cool*) Tell me something further.

YONADAB: Yes, Lord King?

DAVID: How do you know this?

(*Pause.*)

Because you knew it was to happen? Or did you plan it?

YONADAB: My Lord!

DAVID: Oh yes. Yes. Of course. The Watching Man. I have waited many years for this. Always your eyes on me. In the end I knew it would come through you.

YONADAB: (*Frightened*) My Lord, I did not touch him! I swear! My hands are guiltless!

DAVID: And your brains? I know you. Don't strike yourself: make others strike.

(YONADAB *turns away.*)

Do you have sons, Yonadab?

YONADAB: You know I do not.

DAVID: But you can take mine. My firstborn son, whom the Lord allowed me from my thrusting years . . . And what else? What else have you taken from me? Tamar? Was that you also – the spoiling of my girl?

YONADAB: No.

DAVID: Oh yes. I know. I see it!

YONADAB: No!

DAVID: It's in your eyes! . . . What death is harsh enough for that? Speak it yourself.

YONADAB: (*With sudden defiance*) For what? It was you – not I – *you* did it! You! Yourself! Not I!

DAVID: What are you saying?

YONADAB: Who sent your daughter to Amnon – you or I? Who sent your sons to Absalom? (*'Priestly' voice*) 'Go – go, my children! Take my blessing!' Who said that? All-seeing David: what did you see?

(DAVID *stares at him.*)

Yes. It's true. I ruined your family. Yes. But what did they see for you, your eyes? Anointed eyes. Mine are nothing – dim, common eyes – but *yours*! *What you claimed for yours!*

(*Pause.*)

Understand it. I worked it all. Your daughter ruined – your son speared like a boar! And nothing stopped me! *God did nothing*! Just kept you blind and left me to do it! *Understand it!*

(DAVID, *appalled, sinks to the ground.* YONADAB *grows more and more upset.*)

King David, our shield! What shield are you to us? You saw nothing! All I suffered under you! Your pride – your rages – your looks at me every day: everything was bearable if you were *true*. True servant of a true God – seeing more than us. Speaking for us to Him! Loving us to Him! *Without* this, who *are* you – *more than me or anyone*?

(YONADAB *stands over the King, half weeping.*)

Why could you not have seen? Stopped me? Struck me down? SHOWN ME – SHOWN ME HE *IS*?

(*He stares, raging, into* DAVID*'s face. A long moment, then* DAVID *rises.* YONADAB *puts out his hand to help him, but* DAVID *rejects the help. Instead he extends his own right arm in ritual gesture.*)

DAVID: Take this curse for all your life. As the Lord is my Lord, may it stay with you all your days. Be a Watcher and no more, for life. See it as through a veil drawn before your eyes. Be as a dead man in the midst of the living – warmed by nothing. And may my daughter, whom you have brought to such bitterness, bring you a bitterness even beyond death.

(*Stiffly he turns and starts to go out.*)

YONADAB: (*Calling after him, jeering savagely*) Oh terrible! Terrible! Look at me – I'm reduced to ashes! Oh, what power! David the Great has spoken and Yonadab the Nobody is dead! You tell me! – what death is harsh enough for *you*? – ruling us and *blind*!

(*But* DAVID *does not seem to hear. He walks rigidly offstage.* YONADAB *bursts into laughter.*)

(*To audience*) Brilliant old man. Still striving for one last effect! In our day he would have been a man of the theatre, no doubt of it! I stood there intoxicated. What did I care any more? I'd dismissed him! You saw for yourselves: I'm not lying. Ghosts never lie, my dears: they can't. *I had dismissed King David!* Some spirit had lent me a tongue of fire to save my life and scorch his. Suddenly I was without fear – no longer creeping. I was out of Yonadab's world. Upright! . . . Another King was rising. Mercy and gentleness were coming to this quailing People – yes, and perhaps something greater than a King! What might I not see now? All stones put down at last! All arms lifted in joy! Perhaps a young God and Goddess! Who knows what's possible? Leave this Palace of Curses, Yonadab. Go out and greet whatever shall appear!

(*He steps eagerly on to the outer stage. The light changes.*)

Laughing, I stumble out of the city. Take the road they will be coming on: the highway from Ba'al Hazoor. The land is shining! Every Sign is right! It is true – I *am* an Instrument! I have condemned Kings and brought them low. I have beheld Amnon rebuked! Absalom reformed! Tamar reborn! May not Yonadab be reborn also? Now let me see my dream come to pass – a golden man and his golden bride riding under the smile of Heaven, crying Peace in the desert places! *Let it be!* Let this design, begun in lust, flower at last in love!

(*He kneels. Behind his back on the inner stage a curtained litter is approaching, grim and black, supported by Absalom's* GUARDS. *It moves inexorably towards him.*)

Do I bow before a golden calf made by myself? I only know that life here is insupportable. And nothing in myself can change it unhelped. If Spirit needs us to birth it, I am ready. (*Humbly*) Wait in the dust. Receive what you are given.

SCENE FOURTEEN

The litter stops and is set down. The curtains part. We see TAMAR *sitting in it alone.*

YONADAB: (*Alarmed*) Where is he?
(TAMAR *signals to the* GUARDS. *They help her out of the litter.*)
Where is he?!

TAMAR: Fled.

YONADAB: What?

TAMAR: Fled.

YONADAB: Where? Why is he not with you?

TAMAR: He fled.

YONADAB: *How?!*

TAMAR: He came to me after the killing. He said, 'Now, Tamar!'

YONADAB: Yes?
(ABSALOM *enters, bloodstained and smiling. Another Three-cornered Scene begins.* ABSALOM *in the past addresses* TAMAR *and she replies.* YONADAB *remains in the present.*)

ABSALOM: Now! It's time! My love! My sister love! My Queen!
(*He advances and tries to embrace her. She puts out her hand to him. Misunderstanding, he seizes her and embraces her fiercely. She stands unresponsive. He looks at her face. He releases her.*)
What is it?

TAMAR: (*Quiet*) It's over.

ABSALOM: Yes!

TAMAR: All of it. It's finished, Absalom.

ABSALOM: What do you mean?

TAMAR: You have broken your oath to your father, so you are cursed.

ABSALOM: For *you*! I broke it only for you! For us!

TAMAR: You still broke it.

ABSALOM: For us!

TAMAR: So you are cursed. That is all. Run into the desert and hide.

ABSALOM: *What?*

TAMAR: (*Coolly*) Go quickly now, or be killed. That is the choice. These will kill you on my command.

ABSALOM: (*Astounded*) Tamar!

TAMAR: It was your order they obey me. Have you forgotten? (*She laughs*.)

ABSALOM: (*Gently*) The killing has hurt your mind. You're wounded, my dearest girl. I'll heal you!

TAMAR: What? 'Hurt' . . . *I* – hurt? (*She laughs harder*.) Did you say 'hurt'?

ABSALOM: Tamar, *what is it*? I did what you asked me. No more.

TAMAR: Yes.

ABSALOM: So now we can fulfil our plan.

TAMAR: What plan?

ABSALOM: According to the Signs.

TAMAR: What Signs?

ABSALOM: Oh, Tamar – don't play! Remember your dream. You chose me – led through a hundred streets to my love!

TAMAR: (*Coldly*) To your Tower.

ABSALOM: What?

TAMAR: Your Tower. Your house has a tower, Absalom.

(MICAH *appears: in the past*.)

MICAH: (*To* TAMAR) The highest in all the city, Madam.

TAMAR: My maid Micah pointed it out when I came to Amnon in the litter.

MICAH: That is your Absalom's house. The King's gift to him. Isn't it fine?

TAMAR: (*To* MICAH, *smiling*) It's as handsome as he is!

MICAH: Yes indeed, Madam! You cannot mistake it.

TAMAR: (*To* ABSALOM) It is not difficult to find one's way by a tower. A small mystery surely. But of course – (*mischievously*) – when men are determined to believe nonsense there's no preventing them.

ABSALOM: (*Startled*) Where did you hear that? You listened! *You listened to us speaking – Yonadab and me!*

TAMAR: To every word, of course. Behind the curtains.

(YONADAB – *realizing it – cries out*.)

(*To* YONADAB, *with contempt*) *Your* way, isn't it? Hide and overhear?

YONADAB: (*Frantic*) And the dream – my golden dream! You overheard that as well? You never dreamed *that*?

TAMAR: (*Hard*) I never dream at all.

(YONADAB *muffles his face in his robe.* ABSALOM *groans in despair.* MICAH *leaves the stage.*)

(*Savagely, to* ABSALOM) Did you think I would believe such evil? You and I – *Gods?* GODS? There is only One God in Heaven!

(*Pause.*)

How I loathed you when you spoke all that wickedness! I made myself smile at you – kiss the blasphemy on your lips!

ABSALOM: Tamar!

TAMAR: God will forgive me because it was His work I was doing.

ABSALOM: What work? What are you saying? *What work?*

TAMAR: What you wouldn't do. What Father wouldn't. Or anyone.

ABSALOM: (*Understanding*) Destroy Amnon.

TAMAR: Yes.

ABSALOM: Using me to do it.

TAMAR: Yes.

YONADAB: (*Shrieking*) And me! Using me as well! . . . *Me!*

TAMAR: (*Fiercely to him*) All! Any and all!

ABSALOM: Oh no, Tamar . . . No!

TAMAR: (*Bursting out; to* ABSALOM) You took me in. You put your cloak round me and said, 'Justice!' Then you came back with *nothing*! That very night God spoke to me. '*Thou*, Tamar, must do it! What no man will do for me. *Avenge!* . . . I will not suffer Unrighteousness to go unpunished in Israel!'

YONADAB: (*Raising his head*) Ah-ha!

TAMAR: This was His command to me. 'Cleanse the People. Root out iniquity from their midst!'

YONADAB: (*Bitterly*) Oh yes! I see! Of course! . . . And your own vengeance had nothing to do with it?

TAMAR: (*To him*) They are the same. I am God's instrument, no more.

YONADAB: Naturally! . . . David's daughter to the end!

TAMAR: (*Serenely*) I am His right hand, Yonadab. I am His arm.

(ABSALOM *buries his face in his hands and stands rigid.*)

YONADAB: Poor Absalom. Poor, poor man. How he adored you! Poor deluded fool!

TAMAR: As I did him.

YONADAB: You?! You – adore? *You? – Adore?*

TAMAR: (*Crying out*) *I worshipped him!*

(*A pause. She is in huge distress.*)

Do you think it cost me nothing? I wept every night for what I had to do. I cried up to the Lord on high, 'Don't make me! I can't do it!' But He wouldn't yield. 'Do my bidding, Tamar! Do it! *Do it!*' . . . In the end He helped me. He hardened my heart. He showed me there was no difference between the brothers. Not in the end. No difference: Bull or Beauty.

YONADAB: That's not true!

TAMAR: (*Moving round the frozen figure of* ABSALOM.) He was my darling all my childhood, dearest Absalom . . . He loved me purely . . . But when I found refuge in his house that changed. Once I'd been broken by his brother that changed. Suddenly he wanted me too. I saw it. He smelt the blood on me *and he wanted me too*! (*To* ABSALOM) I looked in your face and there was *Amnon*! The Bull was there again!

(ABSALOM *turns away.*)

Run now. Don't make me kill you. I swear I will, if you don't. Run . . . Please . . . Absalom! Run! . . . *Please!* . . . *Please!*

(*But he stands, unable to move.*)

(*To the* GUARDS) Raise your spears. Raise them!

(*Reluctantly they obey her.*)

ABSALOM: No! Lower! I command!

(*They hesitate.*)

Am I heard?

TAMAR: (*To them*) Remember his words to you. 'Cursed is he who breaks this oath.' Well? Obey me now or take that curse. Decide! . . . *Well?*

(*They decide, and raise their spears fully.*)

(*To* ABSALOM) Go now.

(*He stares at her – still barely able to believe it.*)

(*Crying out*) GO!

(*Slowly he turns in final despair and goes off.* TAMAR *stands with her arms flung out in anguish after him.*)

YONADAB: Monstrous . . . Monstrous! . . . He alone was learning to be gentle . . . He was our only hope!

TAMAR: (*Coldly*) There is no hope in man, Yonadab.

YONADAB: There was in *him*! In him there was!

TAMAR: I knew him better. All he really wanted was the throne.

YONADAB: No!

TAMAR: Yes, in the end, that's all! Amnon dead would make it easy. No other rival in sight.

YONADAB: No!

TAMAR: Didn't you hear him? The glee in his voice when he said it? 'Father's days are numbered. The Gods will strike him dead! We just ride into the city and David will *topple*!'

YONADAB: He loved you, Tamar. He loved you!

TAMAR: Yes? What did you think would happen after he'd had me? (*Sarcastic*) Peace and mercy would shine from his eyes for ever? Loving-kindness would fill this tribe? The tribes of Israel and Judah would *learn to be gentle*? (*Coolly*) How long would it have taken him to tire of me? A month? Or just a night, like the other one? Perhaps I'd have been thrown into the street again – the whore who'd had both her great brothers. (*Pause. To the* GUARDS) Quick. Bring Prince Amnon to us.

YONADAB: Amnon? . . . You have him *with* you?

TAMAR: Bring him here! Quickly!

YONADAB: No, Tamar. I beg you!

TAMAR: *Quickly! Bring!*

(*She claps her hands sharply. The* GUARDS *run off. A pause.*)

I *was* guided that morning in the street – whatever you think, I moved under the Lord's hand. Not just for myself but for the People. To take the filth from the tribe . . . Here it is. (*Calling*) Bring the Bull to his friend!

(*The* GUARDS *bring in the bloody and naked body of* AMNON *lying across their poles. They lay it down on the outer stage.* YONADAB *turns away.*)

No, no – look. Thousands saw it today – him slung over a mule, his head under its hole. I said to them who stared, 'This

is Amnon – son of the King. See what has been done to him today by Tamar, daughter of the King – handmaid of the God of Justice! See him – torn as he tore! Gashed as he gashed me! On my eyes when I am old you will still read what they witnessed today: his lips bursting on the hoofs of a mule, dung falling out of the mule on to his eating mouth!' Justice has returned to Israel. I have returned it.
(*She turns to the* GUARDS.)
Go tell it in Jerusalem what has been done today in Ba'al Hazoor. Go – I release you. Tell it to all you meet: Tamar has made Israel whole again. She has sweetened Israel in the nostrils of the Lord! Tell them I am coming. They must greet me with laughter and the instruments of music. Tell them I will make a new Song for them and they shall sing it. I will make a new Song unto the Lord Who is Justice – and He shall be well pleased! Go now. Run to the City! Tell the People they are purified! Tell them they are worthy again to be God's Chosen, who will not suffer iniquity to go unpunished! Go now. Go! I release you. *Go! Go!* GO!
(*She snatches a spear from one of the* GUARDS *and drives them away. They scramble offstage before her blows, taking the litter with them, leaving the body of* AMNON *behind on the ground.* TAMAR *bursts into a high wordless note and stamps the earth in triumph, raising her spear on high. We see a Warrior–Priestess, self-intoxicated. Finally she flings the spear away and sits in the centre of the inner stage.* YONADAB *has watched all this in horrified amazement.* MICAH, *the waiting-woman, re-enters holding a small drum and a stylized, long grey wig. She hands the drum to* TAMAR, *who extends her hands upwards to receive it.*)

YONADAB: Take it – take it, Tamar: your awful triumph. Hold words to your breast instead of lovers! Compose your Song of Righteousness. Let it match Miriam's, the Prophetess – let it match Deborah's, the Prophetess! 'And Tamar the Princess took a timbrel in her hand, and sang unto the women of Israel!'

TAMAR: (*Repeating his last words*) 'And sang unto the women of Israel!'

YONADAB: (*Jeeringly*) *What?*

TAMAR: (*Declaiming from the ground*) 'Behold the Prince was cast down! He was dragged in the dust of the way!'

YONADAB: Not bad!

TAMAR: 'The stones of the way rebuked him. He was carded by the shards of the road!'

YONADAB: Very good! That's exactly the style. Go on!

TAMAR: 'His head was shattered as a winepot. Yea – as a winepot is broken on stones! The feet of the mule did trample: the feet of his sister made dance!'

YONADAB: Beautiful! Absolutely beautiful! They'll all repeat *that*! 'The feet of the mule did trample!'

TAMAR: The feet of his sister made dance!

YONADAB: Perfect!

(TAMAR *strikes the drum harder and repeats the line in a slightly older voice.*)

TAMAR: The feet of the mule did trample: the feet of his sister made dance!

YONADAB: (*Savagely*) Wonderful! That should make you immortal! The Song of Blood-thirst Slaked! A song that shrinks its singer with each repeat. See how at each repeat her legend hardens. Sanctity gathers round her shrivelling form!

(MICAH *crowns her mistress with the great grey wig.*)

TAMAR: (*In an older voice*) The feet of the mule did trample: the feet of his sister made dance! (*Older voice yet*) The feet of the mule did trample: the feet of his sister made dance!

(*She continues to repeat her line to herself, rapt but barely audible, now a crone. The six* HELPERS *come in as* WOMEN *and sit around her.*)

YONADAB: (*To audience*) Women came from all parts of the land to touch her robe. To reverence her with their hands and eyes. And she sat for life in her palace and sang to her savage God, the stink of vengeance the incense of her Faith. She knew more joy in the memory of killing than ever she would have known in the making of children. For life she sat, a Chosen Prophetess, and turned all her pain into meaning. And I sat banished on my dreary estate, and knew *none*. No meaning. Ever. One moment of hope – then dark for ever. No one could abuse me – delude me – disappoint me – ever again. I was totally free. (*Bitterly*) And what song sounded in my head to celebrate the freedom? Silence.

TAMAR: (*Her voice now that of an ancient woman*) The feet of the mule did trample: the feet of his sister made dance! Amen! Selah!

(*Low music sounds. From high above descends the corpse of* ABSALOM *hanging by its long black hair.*)

YONADAB: (*To audience*) Absalom died later – caught in a tree by his famous hair, fleeing the wrath of his father.

(KING DAVID *appears, his head under a prayer shawl. The* HELPERS *depart.*)

The father mourned his eldest son, of course – but the mourning for Absalom far exceeded the mourning for Amnon. It was the hardest pain of his life.

(DAVID *raises his arms.*)

I saw all their transports, this royal family, their lusts for transcendence – and I saw nothing. Always the curtain was between us.

DAVID: O, my son Absalom, my son, my son Absalom!

YONADAB: Always between me and men that curtain of separation.

DAVID: O, my son, my son!

YONADAB: Always on me the curse of that man! (*He points to the King.*) To watch for ever unmoved. To see the *gestures* of faith in others, but no more. The consonants of credulity, but never the vowels which might give its feeling. Tell me – is He not proven to exist, a God whose Priest-King can work this?

DAVID: O, my son Absalom, my son, my son Absalom – *would to God I had died for thee*!

(*All hold their postures. The body of* ABSALOM *turns in the air.*)

YONADAB: David ben Jesse – you are revenged! And your God with you. And Tamar, your terrible, exalted daughter. How I *despised* her! And how I *envied* her! . . . Hateful to me are they who stink of Faith, and murder in its name. But hateful to me as fully are they who bear King David's curse and stink of Nothing. Who have no sustenance beyond themselves.

(*The lights begin to go down.*)

What choice, then, is this? You tell me, my dears. The fanatic

in her blazing simplicity – the sceptic in his chill complexity? Creed and the ruin that makes all over the earth. Or No Creed, and the rape *that* makes. She or me? What choice, I ask you, is this – between Belief and None, where each is lethal?
(*Pause.*)
Yonadab hangs in Yonadab's world, attached to the Tree of Unattachment. Who will cut me down?
(*The lights fade as the* HELPERS *appear and ceremoniously escort* YONADAB *from the stage.*)